Gooseberry Patch

Super-Simple
COMFORT FOODS

Simply delicious family recipes
that are a snap to make!

Gooseberry Patch

An imprint of
The Globe Pequot Publishing Group, Inc.
64 South Main Street
Essex, CT 06426

www.gooseberrypatch.com

1•800•854•6673

Do you have a tried & true recipe...

tip, craft or memory that you'd like to see featured in a **Gooseberry Patch** cookbook? Visit our website at **www.gooseberrypatch.com** and follow the easy steps to submit your favorite family recipe. Or send them to us at:

Gooseberry Patch
PO Box 812
Columbus, OH 43216-0812

Don't forget to include the number of servings your recipe makes, plus your name, address, phone number and email address. If we select your recipe, your name will appear right along with it... and you'll receive a **FREE** copy of the book!

Extra space for recipe if needed:

Tell us about yourself...

Your complete contact information is needed so that we can send you your FREE cookbook, if your recipe is published. Phone numbers and email addresses are kept private and will only be used if we have questions about your recipe.

Name:

Address:

City: State: Zip:

Email:

Daytime Phone:

Thank you! Vickie & Jo Ann

CONTENTS

Dedication

To all of our friends who love to cook favorite comfort foods for family & friends.

Appreciation

A hearty thanks to all of you who shared your tastiest, easiest recipes with us.

Simply Delicious BREAKFASTS

Family-Size Potato Omelet

Carolyn Deckard
Bedford, IN

Not just for breakfast...my family likes this omelet any time of day! It's a great way to use cooked potatoes left over from dinner, too.

6 eggs
2 T. water
1 t. salt, divided
5 T. oil
2 c. cooked redskin potatoes, diced
1 c. onion, chopped
1/2 c. green pepper, chopped
1/4 c. fresh chives, chopped
1/2 t. coarse pepper
Garnish: sour cream

Beat eggs, water and 1/2 teaspoon salt in a large bowl; set aside. Heat oil in a large skillet over medium-high heat; add potatoes, onion, green pepper and chives. Cook, stirring constantly, until potatoes are lightly golden and onion and green pepper are tender. Season with remaining salt and pepper. Reduce heat to medium; pour egg mixture over mixture in skillet. As mixture starts to cook, gently lift edges of omelet with a spatula and tilt pan so uncooked portion flows underneath. Cover and cook for 5 to 6 minutes, until uncooked portion on top sets. Cut into wedges; serve with sour cream. Makes 4 servings.

Looking ahead to a hearty breakfast in the morning? The night before, chop veggies and whisk eggs. Cover in separate bowls and tuck in the refrigerator...breakfast will go together in no time at all!

Ham & Broccoli Quiche

Donna Foley
Omaha, NE

My husband Mike loves quiche, so I adapted this recipe to suit our tastes. Now I love quiche too! It's wonderful for an easy breakfast or for dinner.

3 c. shredded Cheddar cheese, divided
9-inch deep-dish pie crust, unbaked
2 c. cooked ham, chopped
2 c. broccoli, chopped or cut into bite-size flowerets
3 eggs plus 1 egg yolk, well beaten
1-1/4 c. milk

Spread one cup shredded cheese in unbaked pie crust; set aside. Mix together ham and broccoli in a bowl; sprinkle over cheese in crust. Top with remaining cheese; set aside. Whisk together eggs and milk in a bowl; pour over cheese. Bake at 350 degrees for 45 minutes to one hour, until a knife tip inserted in the center comes out clean. Let stand for 5 to 10 minutes; cut into wedges. Makes 8 servings.

Make a quick, savory crumb crust for a quiche. Spread 2-1/2 tablespoons softened butter in a pie plate, then firmly press 2-1/2 cups crisp cracker crumbs into the butter. Freeze until firm, spoon in filling and bake as directed.

Scrumptious Apple Baked Oatmeal

Karen Antonides
Gahanna, OH

This delicious oatmeal is wonderful on a cold day, served with a little maple syrup on top. I use Honey Crisp apples because they are my favorite, but any good baking apple will do. I serve this to holiday guests and it is a wonderful way to start the day.

3 c. milk
3 T. pure maple syrup
2 T. butter, melted
1 egg, beaten
1 t. baking powder
2 t. vanilla extract
2 t. pumpkin pie spice
1/4 t. salt
2 c. rolled oats, uncooked
2 c. Honey Crisp apples, cored and chopped
Optional: 1/2 c. chopped walnuts, divided

In a large bowl, combine all ingredients except oats, apples and optional walnuts; whisk well. Stir in oats, apples and 1/4 cup walnuts, if using. Spoon mixture into a greased 8"x8" baking pan. Bake, uncovered, at 350 degrees for about 45 to 55 minutes, until puffed and center is just set. Sprinkle with remaining walnuts during last 5 minutes of baking, if using. Serve warm. Leftovers may be covered and refrigerated for 3 to 4 days; reheat in microwave with a little additional milk splashed on top. Makes 4 to 6 servings.

Fill a muffin tin with yummy oatmeal toppings...brown sugar, raisins, chopped nuts and even chocolate chips. So easy for everyone to help themselves! The muffin tin can be wrapped in plastic, for serving again another day.

Simply Delicious BREAKFASTS

Fluffy Pancakes

Gloria Kaufmann
Orrville, OH

Our favorite go-to pancake recipe. I always use bread flour for this recipe. Serve with plenty of butter and your favorite syrup!

1 c. bread flour
2 T. sugar
1-1/2 t. baking powder
1/2 t. salt
1 egg
1/4 c. oil
3/4 c. milk

Combine bread flour, sugar, baking powder and salt in a bowl; mix well. In another bowl, beat egg, oil and milk. Add flour mixture and stir, but do not overmix. Let stand for 5 minutes while heating a greased griddle over medium heat. Add batter to griddle, 1/4 cup at a time. Cook until bubbles form; flip to other side and cook until golden. Serves 3.

Easy Berry Salad

Nancy Wise
Little Rock, AR

Spoon these delectable berries over yogurt, hot oatmeal or your favorite cereal, or simply enjoy as is!

1 c. fresh strawberries, hulled and halved or quartered
1 c. fresh blueberries
1 c. fresh blackberries
1 c. fresh raspberries
1 t. sugar, or to taste

Combine all berries in a bowl. Sprinkle with sugar; mix gently. Serves 4 to 6.

Cut up pancakes in a jiffy using a pizza cutter.

Holiday Egg Bake

Lynne Doughan
Britt, IA

At our house, this delicious egg bake was made not only for company, but for all our family holidays...Easter, Thanksgiving, Christmas, New Year's Day, birthdays and anniversaries. It's always requested when all the kids are home.

1 doz. eggs
1/4 c. fresh parsley, chopped
2 T. butter
salt and pepper to taste
28-oz. pkg. frozen diced potatoes with onions & peppers
1-1/4 c. sour cream
1 lb. diced cooked ham or browned ground pork sausage
Optional: 2 4-oz. cans sliced mushrooms, drained
8-oz. pkg. shredded sharp Cheddar cheese

Whisk together eggs and parsley in a large bowl. Melt butter in a very large skillet over medium heat; add eggs, salt and pepper. Scramble just to the moist stage; do not overcook. Meanwhile, spray a 13"x9" deep baking pan with non-stick vegetable spray. Spread frozen potatoes in pan; season with salt and pepper. Spoon scrambled eggs over hashbrowns; dollop with sour cream and spread evenly over eggs. Top with ham or sausage, mushrooms if using and shredded cheese. Cover and refrigerate overnight. Bake, covered, at 350 degrees for 45 to 50 minutes, until eggs are set and cheese is melted. Makes 10 servings.

Treat everyone to buttery slices of cinnamon toast. Spread softened butter generously on one side of toasted white bread and sprinkle with cinnamon-sugar. Broil for one to 2 minutes, until bubbly and golden. Yum!

Simply Delicious BREAKFASTS

Bev's Pineapple-Banana Loaf

Bev Traxler
British Columbia, Canada

This fruit-filled bread can be served as breakfast or dessert. It is a great hit at the annual bake sale. Freezes well and the best thing is, the recipe makes two loaves!

3 c. all-purpose flour
2 c. sugar
1 t. baking powder
1 t. baking soda
1 t. salt
1 c. canned crushed pineapple with juice
3 eggs, beaten
1-1/2 c. canola oil
2 c. ripe bananas, mashed
2 t. vanilla extract

Combine flour, sugar, baking powder, baking soda and salt in a large bowl; mix well and set aside. In a separate bowl, beat together undrained pineapple and remaining ingredients until well blended. Add flour mixture and stir until thoroughly combined. Divide batter between 2 greased 8-1/2"x4-1/2" loaf pans, spreading evenly. Bake at 350 degrees for 60 to 70 minutes, until a toothpick inserted in the center comes out clean. Cool in pans for 15 minutes; remove to a wire rack and cool completely. Makes 2 loaves.

Need a gift in a jiffy for a teacher, a neighbor or a friend with a new baby? Give a loaf of freshly baked quick bread wrapped in a pretty tea towel...it's sure to be appreciated.

Super-Simple COMFORT FOODS

Grandma's Berry French Toast

Paula Marchesi
Auburn, PA

I have loved French toast since I was a little girl, and this recipe was my grandmother's. My mom made this in various ways every Sunday after church. With the jewel tones of sweet and tart berries, it was simply out-of-this-world scrumptiously delicious, and it's so easy to make the night before. I don't make it every Sunday, but at least every other Sunday. Enjoy!

1-lb. loaf French bread, cubed
6 eggs
1-1/2 c. milk
1 t. sugar
1 t. cinnamon
1/2 t. salt
1 t. vanilla extract
12-oz. pkg. frozen mixed berries
2 t. cold butter
1/2 c. brown sugar, packed

Spread bread cubes in a 13"x9" baking pan coated with non-stick vegetable spray; set aside. Beat eggs in a large bowl; whisk in milk, sugar, cinnamon, salt and vanilla. Pour egg mixture over bread cubes in pan. Cover and refrigerate overnight. In the morning, let French toast in pan and frozen berries stand at room temperature while preheating the oven. Bake, covered, at 350 degrees for 30 minutes. In a bowl, cut butter into brown sugar until crumbly. Top French toast with berries; sprinkle with brown sugar mixture. Bake, uncovered, for 15 to 20 minutes longer, until a knife tip inserted in the center comes out clean. Let stand for 5 minutes before serving. Makes 8 servings.

Don't hesitate to use day-old bread for making French toast... it absorbs the milk so much better than bakery-fresh bread.

Simply Delicious BREAKFASTS

Impossible Quiche

Linda Finfrock
Cary, NC

An easy recipe I've made for years...it's quick & easy during the busy holiday season, or anytime. Instead of bacon, you can use 1/2 cup ground pork sausage, browned and drained, or 1/2 cup cooked ham, diced. Add your favorite veggies as you please, too!

1/2 c. bacon, crisply cooked and crumbled
1/3 c. onion, finely chopped
1 c. shredded Cheddar or Swiss cheese
2 c. milk
1/2 c. biscuit baking mix
4 eggs
1/4 t. salt
1/8 t. pepper

Sprinkle crumbled bacon, onion and cheese evenly into a lightly greased 9" or 10" pie plate. Combine remaining ingredients in a blender; process on high speed for one minute. Pour into pie plate. Bake at 350 degrees for 50 to 55 minutes, until golden and a knife inserted in center comes out clean. Let stand 5 minutes before cutting into wedges. Makes 6 servings.

Rice-Cooker Grits

Sandra Turner
Fayetteville, NC

As a southerner, I have always enjoyed grits. Since making breakfast can be overwhelming, frying the meat and cooking the eggs, I decided to try making my grits in the rice cooker, using the same instructions as on the grits container. It was a huge success! I have made them this way ever since.

3 c. water
3/4 c. quick-cooking grits, uncooked
1/4 t. salt
butter to taste

Add water, grits and salt to a rice cooker; stir to combine. Cover and set rice cooker to cook. When rice cooker turns off or turns to warm (depending on your cooker), stir in butter and serve. Makes 4 servings.

Overnight Cinnamon Rolls

Jenny Bishoff
Oakland, MD

I came up with this variation on cinnamon rolls when I had some frozen pizza dough I needed to use. It worked well, and I liked not having to make dough from scratch!

1-lb. ball pizza dough
1/2 c. butter, softened and divided
1/2 c. brown sugar, packed, or to taste
1 to 2 t. cinnamon
1/2 c. whipped cream cheese
1 t. vanilla extract
1 c. powdered sugar
2 to 3 T. milk

Roll out pizza dough into a 12-inch by 8-inch rectangle on a lightly floured surface. Spread with 6 tablespoons butter; sprinkle with brown sugar and cinnamon to taste. Roll up dough, starting on one long side; slice into 9 rolls. Arrange rolls in a greased 9"x9" baking pan and cover with plastic wrap. Refrigerate overnight to rise. In the morning, uncover; allow to come to room temperature while oven is preheating. Bake at 375 degrees for 30 to 35 minutes, until golden. Meanwhile, stir together remaining butter, cream cheese and vanilla until smooth. Stir in powdered sugar and enough milk to create a spreading consistency. Spread icing over rolls while still warm. Makes 9 rolls.

Write or paste your most-used recipes on index cards...they'll fit perfectly into a flip photo album. You'll easily find the recipe you want, and the plastic pages will protect recipes from spatters.

Simply Delicious BREAKFASTS

Fruity Cheese Danish

Missy Abbott
Hickory, PA

My husband loves cheese danish, and so when pressed for time, I whip this simple recipe up for him. He has no idea it wasn't made from scratch!

8-oz. pkg. cream cheese, softened
1/4 c. sugar
1 t. vanilla extract
2 16.3-oz. tubes refrigerated jumbo biscuits
21-oz. can favorite fruit pie filling

Blend together cream cheese, sugar and vanilla in a bowl; set aside. Separate biscuits. Slice or split each biscuit horizontally to make 2 biscuits out of each one. Arrange biscuits on a parchment paper-lined baking sheet. Use a spoon to make a little well in the center of each biscuit. Spoon one teaspoon of cream cheese mixture onto each biscuit; spread around. Top each biscuit with one teaspoon pie filling. Bake at 350 degrees for 12 to 14 minutes, until lightly golden. Cool; drizzle with glaze, if desired. Makes 32 danish.

Optional Glaze:

1/2 c. powdered sugar
1-1/2 T. milk
1/4 t. vanilla extract

Mix all ingredients, adding enough milk for a glaze consistency.

Save time on kitchen clean-up...use a spatter screen when frying in a skillet or Dutch oven.

Super-Simple COMFORT FOODS

Sausage & Mushroom Quiche

Darrell Lawry
Kissimmee, FL

It's easy to change the ingredients for this tasty quiche! Try crispy bacon instead of sausage and swap out the cheese, too.

1 lb. ground pork sausage
4 eggs, beaten
1/2 c. milk
1/2 c. mayonnaise
1 T. cornstarch
1/4 t. salt
1/4 t. pepper
8-oz. pkg. shredded Cheddar cheese
4-oz. can mushroom stems & pieces, drained
9-inch pie crust, unbaked

Brown sausage in a skillet over medium heat; drain well. Meanwhile, in a large bowl, combine eggs, milk, mayonnaise, cornstarch, salt, pepper and cheese; mix well. Stir in mushrooms and sausage. Spoon mixture into unbaked pie crust. Bake at 400 degrees for 25 to 35 minutes, until puffy and golden. Let stand for 10 minutes; cut into wedges. Makes 6 servings.

Parmesan Egg in a Hole

Zoe Bennett
Columbia, SC

An old-fashioned favorite, jazzed up with Parmesan cheese.

1/3 c. mayonnaise
1/4 c. grated Parmesan cheese
4 slices white bread
4 eggs
salt and pepper to taste

Stir together mayonnaise and cheese in a small bowl. Spread mixture onto both sides of each bread slice. With a small glass, cut a circle in the center of each bread slice. Working in batches, in a large skillet over medium heat, cook bread until golden on one side. Turn over; break an egg into the center of each slice. Sprinkle with seasonings. Reduce heat to medium-low and cook for 3 to 4 minutes, until eggs are set. Remove to serving plates. Cook bread circles until golden on both sides; serve alongside bread slices. Makes 4 servings.

For the fluffiest scrambled eggs ever, try Grandma's secret... stir in a pinch of baking powder!

Italian Strata

Margaret Welder
Madrid, IA

The original recipe for this dish came from a friend's mother, and I adapted it to fit my family's likes. I have taken it often to gatherings and it is always liked. Use half hot sausage and half mild, if you wish.

1 lb. Italian ground pork sausage
1 c. onion, diced
1/2 c. green pepper, diced
14-1/2 oz. can diced tomatoes, drained
3 eggs
2-1/2 c. milk
1 t. salt
1/2 loaf Italian bread, sliced 1/4-inch thick and divided
2 T. grated Parmesan cheese

Brown sausage in a skillet over medium heat; drain and return to skillet. Add onion and green pepper; cook for 5 minutes. Add tomatoes and simmer for 15 minutes, or until liquid has evaporated; remove from heat. Beat eggs, milk and salt in a bowl; set aside. Arrange half of bread slices in a greased deep 13"x9" baking pan; cover with sausage mixture. Top with remaining bread slices; pour egg mixture over the top, covering all of the bread. Sprinkle with cheese. Cover with aluminum foil; refrigerate overnight. Uncover and bake at 325 degrees for one hour. Let stand for 10 minutes before serving. Makes 8 servings.

Poached eggs, easy! For each egg, add one tablespoon water to a muffin cup; break egg directly into cup. Bake at 350 degrees, 11 to 13 minutes for runny yolks, a bit longer for firmer yolks. Remove from oven and let stand for one minute, then gently remove eggs with a slotted spoon.

Blueberry & Caramel Coffee Cake

Marsha Baker
Palm Harbor, FL

I love using shortcuts like canned biscuits! This is a delicious combo of flavors...it will be sure to bring raves.

16.3-oz. tube refrigerated jumbo biscuits
1/2 c. brown sugar, packed
3 T. butter, melted
3/4 t. cinnamon
3/4 c. quick-cooking oats, uncooked and divided
1-1/2 c. fresh or frozen blueberries
1/4 c. sugar
2 T. butter, diced

Separate biscuits; cut into 4 to 8 pieces each. In a generously greased 11"x8" baking pan, arrange biscuit pieces in a single layer as much as possible. Set aside. In a small bowl, combine brown sugar, melted butter and cinnamon. Spoon over biscuits; sprinkle with 1/2 cup oats. In another bowl, combine blueberries and sugar; toss until coated evenly. Spoon over oats and biscuits. Sprinkle with remaining oats; dot with butter. Bake, uncovered, at 375 degrees for about 25 to 30 minutes, until golden. Serve warm. Best reheated in oven, not microwave. Serves 6 to 8.

Try steel-cut oats in recipes that call for regular long-cooking oats. Steel-cut oats are less processed, for a pleasing chewy texture you're sure to enjoy.

Simply Delicious BREAKFASTS

Georgia's Strawberry Bread

Judy Phelan
Macomb, IL

The recipe for this yummy bread came from my sister-in-law Georgia. She is a fabulous cook and baker.

3 c. all-purpose flour
1 t. baking soda
1 t. salt
2 t. cinnamon
4 eggs, beaten
1-1/2 c. oil
2 c. sugar
2 10-oz. pkgs. frozen sliced strawberries, thawed

In a large bowl, mix flour, baking soda, salt and cinnamon. Add eggs, oil and sugar; mix thoroughly. Stir in undrained strawberries. Divide batter evenly between 2 greased and floured 9"x5" loaf pans. Bake at 350 degrees for 35 to 45 minutes. Cool in pan for 10 minutes; remove loaves and cool on a wire rack. Makes 2 loaves.

Whip up a crock of fruit butter to go with warm muffins...yum! Simply blend 1/2 cup each of softened butter and strawberry, apricot or peach preserves.

Comforting Breakfast Bake

Carina Furia
Wayland, NY

My late mother used to serve this make-ahead egg dish every Christmas. Now I make it for my kids and they look forward to it every year. It's really too good to enjoy just once a year!

1 lb. sliced bacon
1 doz. eggs
1/2 c. milk
salt and pepper to taste
2 to 3 T. butter or oil
1/2 c. sour cream
1 c. shredded Cheddar cheese

Cook bacon in a large skillet over medium heat until crisp; drain well and chop or crumble. Meanwhile, combine eggs, milk, salt and pepper in a very large bowl; whisk thoroughly. Heat butter or oil in another large skillet over medium heat. Add egg mixture; cook just until lightly scrambled as desired. Spoon eggs into a buttered 13"x9" baking pan; mix in sour cream. Top with cheese and bacon. Cover and refrigerate overnight. In the morning, uncover. Bake at 350 degrees for 45 minutes, or until heated through and eggs are set. Makes 8 servings.

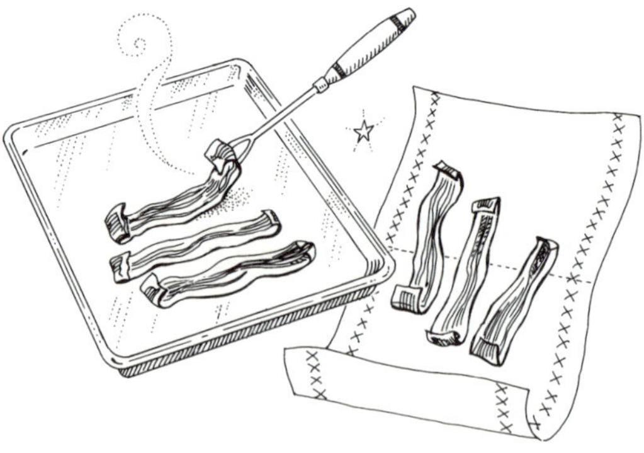

Bacon is tasty at breakfast or anytime, and here's an easy way to fix it. Arrange bacon slices on a rimmed baking sheet and bake at 350 degrees. It'll be crisp in about 15 minutes...no messy spatters!

Simply Delicious BREAKFASTS

Creamy Vanilla French Toast

JoAnn
Gooseberry Patch

Really yummy! Be sure to use cook & serve pudding, not instant.

1 c. whole milk
1 egg, beaten
3-oz. pkg. cook & serve vanilla pudding mix
1/2 t. cinnamon
8 slices Texas toast
1 T. butter
Garnish: powdered sugar, sliced strawberries

In a shallow bowl, combine milk, egg, dry pudding mix and cinnamon. Whisk for 2 minutes, or until well blended. Dip slices of toast into pudding mixture, coating both sides. Melt butter in a large skillet over medium heat. Cook toast on both sides until golden. Garnish as desired and serve. Makes 4 servings.

Dutch Baby

Rise Briggs
Roseburg, OR

This puffy baked pancake is not sweet, so you can add fresh berries, bananas and syrup. Or, you can make it savory with crumbled cooked bacon, melted cheese, tomatoes and peppers, etc.

2 eggs, beaten
1/2 c. milk
1/2 c. all-purpose flour
Garnish: favorite toppings

Stir together eggs, milk and flour until well blended. Pour batter into a buttered 10" glass pie plate. Bake at 500 degrees for 10 minutes; pancake will puff up, then fall. Shake carefully out of the pan. Cut into wedges and add toppings as desired. Serves 2 to 4.

Come and share a pot of tea,
my home is warm and
my friendship's free.
– Emilie Barnes

Irresistible Cinnamon Rolls

Debra Arch
Kewanee, IL

For decades, I used to make my homemade cinnamon rolls from scratch that would require three or more hours from start to finish. This recipe is my new favorite, because it makes rich, gooey delicious cinnamon rolls in less than one hour!

2 17-1/2 oz. tubes refrigerated jumbo cinnamon rolls with cream cheese frosting
1 c. whipping cream
1/2 c. butter, melted
1 c. light brown sugar, packed
2 t. cinnamon
2 t. vanilla extract

Open tubes of rolls; set aside frosting containers. Arrange rolls in a greased 13"x9" baking pan. (I put a vertical column of 2 rolls at each end and 2 vertical columns of 3 rolls in center of pan.) With your hand, press rolls down in pan to spread out. Spoon cream evenly over rolls; set aside. Whisk together remaining ingredients in a bowl; dollop over rolls by tablespoonfuls. Bake, uncovered, at 350 degrees for 25 to 30 minutes. Remove from oven. Allow to cool for 10 minutes; spread reserved frosting over rolls. Makes 10 rolls.

Breakfast sliders! Whip up your favorite pancake batter and make silver dollar-size pancakes. Sandwich them together with warmed heat & serve sausage patties. Serve with maple syrup on the side for dipping...yum!

Simply Delicious BREAKFASTS

Whirly Whirls Butterscotch Biscuits

Amy Theisen
Sauk Rapids, MN

Mom made these butterscotch biscuits quite often for our family of nine. I was the youngest of seven kids, and I remember calling them: Whirly Whirls. Still a family favorite with a warm cup of coffee! They're easily made from scratch...you probably have the ingredients in your pantry.

3 c. all-purpose flour
4-1/2 t. baking powder
3/4 t. salt
3/8 c. plus 1/2 c. butter, divided
1 c. milk
1 c. brown sugar, packed

Mix flour, baking powder and salt in a large bowl. Add 3/8 cup butter; stir with a fork until fine crumbs form. Gradually stir in milk to make a firm dough. Knead dough on a floured surface for 30 seconds; roll dough out to 1/3-inch thick. Blend remaining butter and brown sugar in a bowl; spread over dough. Tightly roll up dough lengthwise; cut into 24 slices, 1/2-inch thick. Cover a baking sheet with aluminum foil; spray with non-stick baking spray and arrange rolls on pan. Bake at 400 degrees for 20 minutes, watching closely to avoid burning. Makes 2 dozen.

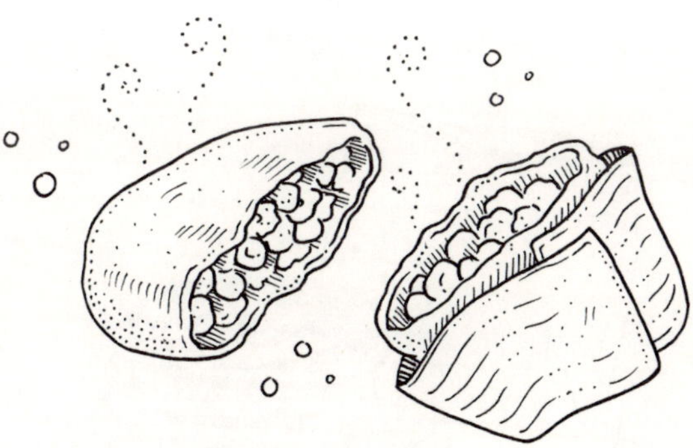

Is the kids' school bus on the way? Fill a pita pocket with a favorite breakfast food...scrambled eggs, a sausage patty and cheese or even sliced bananas with peanut butter. Wrap it up in a paper napkin and they're set to go!

Peaches & Cream Waffles

Lisa McClelland
Columbus, OH

This was my dad's favorite and I would make it for him for Fathers' Day and for his birthday. Dad had developed a fondness for canned peaches while in the Navy and this was a novel way to serve them!

1 c. whole milk
1 c. sour cream
2 eggs, beaten
3 T. butter, melted
1-1/2 t. vanilla extract
1-1/2 c. all-purpose flour
2 t. baking powder
1 t. baking soda
1/2 t. apple pie spice
1/8 t. coarse sea salt
15-1/2 oz. can sliced peaches in heavy syrup, drained and syrup reserved
Garnish: whipped cream

In a large bowl, combine milk, sour cream, eggs, melted butter and vanilla. Beat with an electric mixer on medium speed until well mixed. In another large bowl, combine flour, baking powder, baking soda, spice and salt. Stir milk mixture into flour mixture until batter is smooth. Chop peach slices into small pieces; measure 3/4 cup chopped peaches and set aside any remaining slices for topping. Add chopped peaches to batter and stir to combine. Coat a waffle maker with butter or non-stick vegetable spray. Add batter to preheated waffle maker by cupfuls, or as manufacturer directs. Close lid and bake until a golden crust forms. Serve waffles warm, topped with whipped cream, reserved peach slices and reserved peach syrup. Makes 4 servings.

Freeze leftover waffles and pancakes on a baking sheet, then store in plastic freezer bags for up to a month. Reheat them in a toaster for a quick breakfast.

Baked Blueberry-Almond Oatmeal

Joanne Novellino
Bayville, NJ

Get creative with the add-ins! Instead of blueberries and almonds, try peaches and coconut. Serve topped with milk or cream...yum!

2 eggs, beaten
1-1/2 c. milk
1/4 c. brown sugar, packed
1/4 c. butter, melted
1-1/2 t. baking powder
3 c. rolled oats, uncooked
1 t. cinnamon
1 t. almond or vanilla extract
1/4 t. salt
1/3 c. sliced almonds
1 c. fresh or frozen blueberries

Stir all ingredients together in a large bowl. Spoon batter into a greased 8"x8" glass baking pan. Bake at 350 degrees for 30 to 35 minutes; cut into squares and serve. Makes 9 servings.

Enjoy fresh blueberries year 'round...just freeze them during berry season! Spread ripe berries in a single layer on a baking sheet and freeze until solid, then store them in plastic freezer bags. Later, pour out just the amount you need.

Super-Simple COMFORT FOODS

Denver Omelet Sandwich

Lynda Hart
Bluffdale, UT

My dad loved Denver omelets, so one day Mom made them for breakfast, but we were delayed in eating. So Mom toasted some sandwich buns and served the omelets as sandwiches. I loved them because I could grab one as I went out the door to go to school.

1 T. butter
1/4 c. onion, minced
1/4 c. green pepper, minced
4 eggs, beaten
1/4 c. milk
salt and pepper to taste
1/2 c. cooked ham, minced
4 sandwich buns, split, or 8 slices bread, toasted and buttered

Melt butter in a skillet over medium heat. Add onion and green pepper; sauté until tender. Meanwhile, in a large bowl, whisk together eggs, milk, salt and pepper; stir in ham. Add to onion mixture in pan; scramble until set. Spoon egg mixture onto hot toasted buns or bread and serve. Makes 4 servings.

Pigs in a Muffin

Jennifer Dorward
Winder, GA

We like blueberry pancake mix, but you can use whatever flavor you prefer. You could even use a prepackaged muffin mix instead. Dip in maple syrup or your choice of jam or jelly. Great on the go!

8 brown & serve pork breakfast sausage links
2 c. pancake mix
1-1/3 c. milk

Brown sausages according to package directions; set aside to cool until easily handled. Cut each sausage into 3 pieces; set aside. Meanwhile, in a large bowl, mix pancake mix and milk until smooth. Add one tablespoonful batter to each of 24 greased mini muffin pans. Add one piece of sausage to the center of each muffin. Bake at 350 degrees for 12 to 15 minutes. Makes 2 dozen.

Sausage, Egg & Cheese Roll

Kathleen Salam
Wilmington, DE

I've made this for over 20 years, and people always love it! It's very easy...you can make it a day before and bake it just before serving. It looks impressive, too. Instead of sausage, cooked and crumbled bacon works well.

12.4-oz. tube refrigerated pizza dough
8-oz. pkg. ground pork breakfast sausage
1 to 2 T. butter
4 to 6 eggs, beaten
8-oz. pkg. shredded Cheddar cheese

Set out pizza dough at room temperature to soften. Brown and crumble sausage in a skillet over medium heat; drain well. Melt butter in another skillet over medium heat. Add eggs and scramble as desired, just until set. Unroll pizza dough into a greased 13"x9" baking pan. Spoon sausage and eggs onto center of dough; spread out evenly to both ends. Top with cheese. Carefully roll up dough starting on one long edge so dough folds over, keeping filling inside. Bake, uncovered, at 375 degrees for 20 minutes, or until golden. Cool; slice to serve. Makes 6 to 8 servings.

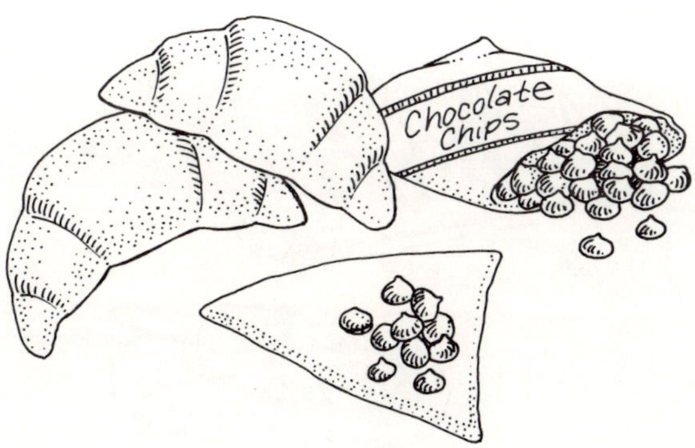

Chocolate croissants in a jiffy! Separate a tube of refrigerated crescent rolls into triangles. Top each triangle with 10 chocolate chips and roll it up. Bake on an ungreased baking sheet at 375 degrees until golden, 12 to 14 minutes. Serve warm.

Crystal's Orange Zucchini Bread

Crystal Shook
Catawba, NC

A delicious fruity bread that's even healthier with zucchini! Make these in muffin pans and they're great for a quick breakfast... just need to bake for 10 to 15 minutes.

3 c. all-purpose flour
1/4 t. baking powder
1 t. baking soda
1 t. salt
1 t. cinnamon
1/2 t. ground cloves
3 eggs, beaten
2 c. sugar
1 c. oil
1 T. orange flavoring or extract
2 c. zucchini, grated

In a large bowl, combine flour, baking powder, baking soda, salt and spices; stir well. Add remaining ingredients; stir until well blended. Divide batter evenly between 2 well-greased and floured 9"x5" loaf pans. Bake at 350 degrees for 50 to 60 minutes. Remove from pans to a wire rack and let cool. Makes 2 loaves.

Make banana pops for breakfast! Insert treat sticks in ripe bananas. Spread with fruit-flavored yogurt, roll in cereal and place on a tray to freeze. Wrap in plastic wrap and return to freezer...a cool treat kids are sure to love.

Julie's Quick Blueberry-Banana Muffins

Julie Dossantos
Fort Pierce, FL

This is a quick & easy recipe to make for a yummy breakfast or after-school snack. Don't forget a glass of cold milk!

15-1/4 oz. pkg. butter yellow cake mix
1 t. baking powder
2 ripe bananas, mashed
3 eggs, beaten
2/3 c. oil
1/3 c. water
1 c. fresh blueberries, divided

Mix together dry cake mix and baking powder in a large bowl; set aside. In another bowl, mix together bananas, eggs, oil, water and 2/3 cup blueberries. Add banana mixture to cake mixture; stir until moistened. Scoop batter into paper-lined muffin cups by 1/2 cupfuls. Top each muffin with a few remaining blueberries, gently pushing berries halfway into batter. Bake at 375 degrees for 15 to 17 minutes. Remove muffins to a wire rack; allow to cool for 15 minutes and serve. Makes 1-1/2 dozen.

Baker's secret! Grease muffin cups on the bottoms and just halfway up the sides. Muffins will bake up nicely puffed on top.

Scrumptious Breakfast Casserole

Laura Fredlund
Papillion, NE

This breakfast is so delicious...it'll make any morning feel a little extra special! Enjoy with a nice bowl of fruit salad and your loved ones.

1 lb. ground hot pork sausage
4 c. frozen shredded hashbrowns
8-oz. pkg. shredded Cheddar cheese
5 green onions, sliced
1 doz. eggs
3/4 c. milk
1-1/2 t. kosher salt
pepper to taste

Brown and crumble sausage in a skillet over medium heat; drain well. In a lightly greased 13"x9" baking pan, layer hashbrowns, cheese, sausage and onions; stir to mix. In a large bowl, whisk together eggs, milk, salt and pepper; pour over mixture in pan. Bake, uncovered, at 350 degrees for 45 minutes, or until eggs are set and cheese is melted. Makes 6 to 8 servings.

Catsup is tasty with eggs and potatoes, but to really wake everyone up at breakfast time, add some spicy salsa or hot pepper sauce!

Simply Delicious BREAKFASTS

Easy Bacon Frittata

Sharon Tillman
Hampton, VA

A classic...oh-so simple to make, tasty either hot or cold. If you don't have an oven-proof skillet, assemble the ingredients in a buttered 9"x9" baking pan. Add a little diced red pimento for color.

6 slices bacon
6 eggs
1 c. milk
2 T. butter, melted
1/2 t. salt
1/4 t. pepper
1/4 c. green onions, chopped
1 c. shredded Cheddar cheese

Cook bacon in a cast-iron skillet over medium heat until crisp, about 10 minutes. Drain bacon on paper towels; partially drain drippings from skillet. In a large bowl, whisk together eggs, milk, melted butter, salt, and pepper; pour into same skillet. Top egg mixture with onions, crumbled bacon and shredded cheese. Bake, uncovered, at 350 degrees for 25 to 30 minutes, until eggs are set and a knife tip inserted near the center comes out clean. Serves 6.

No time for a leisurely breakfast? Try breakfast for dinner... it's sure to become a family favorite!

Streusel Muffins

Vickie
Gooseberry Patch

These wonderful muffins are always a hit at brunch with family & friends...simple to make, too!

1-3/4 c. all-purpose flour
1/3 c. sugar
2 t. baking powder
1/4 t. salt
1 egg, beaten
3/4 c. milk
1/4 c. oil

In a large bowl, combine flour, sugar, baking powder and salt; mix well. Make a well in the center and set aside. In another bowl, whisk together egg, milk and oil. Add egg mixture to flour mixture; stir just until moistened. Batter will be lumpy. Spoon batter into 12 paper-lined or greased muffin cups, filling 2/3 full. Sprinkle evenly with Streusel Topping. Bake at 400 degrees for 18 to 20 minutes, until golden and a toothpick tests clean. Cool in pan on a wire rack for 5 minutes. Remove from muffin cups; serve warm. Makes one dozen.

Streusel Topping:

3 T. all-purpose flour
3 T. butter
2 T. chopped walnuts

Stir together flour and butter until mixture resembles coarse crumbs. Stir in walnuts.

A jar of honey is a sweet addition at breakfast, to enjoy on hot toast or drizzle into hot tea. If the honey has crystallized, simply set the jar in a pan of hot water...it will be ready to use again in just a few minutes.

Tummy-Warming SOUPS & BREADS

Country Cozy Dump Chili

Jenna Harmon
Dolores, CO

Since I developed this chili recipe for the crockpot, everyone who has tried it asks for the recipe! It's perfect for cooler autumn and winter evenings, or if you are like us, we eat chili all year long.

2 lbs. ground beef
1 c. onion, chopped
2 cloves garlic, minced
2 T. chili powder
1-1/2 t. ground cumin
1/2 t. salt
1 t. pepper
28-oz. can diced tomatoes
15-oz. can tomato sauce
2 14-1/2 oz. cans pinto beans in chili sauce
14-1/2 oz. can Great Northern beans
14-1/2 oz. can kidney beans
Garnish: sour cream, cheese, chopped onions, oyster crackers or corn chips

Brown beef in a large skillet over medium heat. Add onion, garlic and seasonings; cook until onion is translucent. Drain; transfer beef mixture to a 6-quart slow cooker. Mix in canned ingredients; do not drain. Stir well. Cover and cook on low setting for 3 hours. Garnish bowls of chili as desired. Serves 8.

Thinking of a crockpot soup for tomorrow's dinner? Ingredients can be browned, chopped and measured as needed, covered and refrigerated. In the morning, it'll be a snap to put your soup together...set the crock and go!

Tummy-Warming SOUPS & BREADS

Quickie Ham & Bean Soup

Elaine Divis
Sioux City, IA

This recipe is an easy way to use up some of that leftover holiday ham. It is quick, easy and makes the perfect amount for a small family. But you can always add more of the veggies and an extra can of beans to customize it for your family.

2 T. butter
2 carrots, peeled and sliced
3 stalks celery, sliced
1/2 c. onion, diced
1/2 t. garlic, minced
4 c. chicken broth
2 c. cooked ham, diced
2 14-1/2 oz. cans Great Northern beans, drained and rinsed
1 bay leaf

Melt butter in a skillet over medium heat; sauté vegetables until softened. Stir in remaining ingredients. Cook for 15 to 20 minutes, stirring occasionally, until vegetables are tender. Discard bay leaf and serve. Makes 4 servings.

Sour Cream Cornbread

Sandy Coffey
Cincinnati, OH

Goes great with your choice of beans! Navy, pinto, 15-bean mixed, lima, etc. Finely chopped green onions, sweet pepper and crumbled bacon can be added, if you like.

14-3/4 oz. can cream-style corn
8-oz. container sour cream
1 c. self-rising cornmeal
2 eggs, beaten
1/4 c. oil

In a large bowl, mix all ingredients well. Pour batter into a greased 9" cast-iron skillet. Bake at 425 degrees for 35 minutes, or until golden. Cool slightly; cut into wedges. Makes 6 servings.

Save bacon drippings in a jar in the fridge. Just a spoonful adds flavor to beans or vegetables, or use them to coat the pan for cornbread.

Crockpot Vegetable Beef Soup

Sandy Durham
Wichita Falls, TX

This simple recipe has been passed on throughout our family. The beef and vegetables slow-cook together to make this a flavorful, hearty dinner that will satisfy everyone. Use more or less beef to suit yourself.

2 lbs. beef round steak, diced
14-1/2 oz. can petite diced tomatoes
2 to 3 Yukon Gold potatoes, peeled and diced
3 carrots, peeled and diced
2 onions, chopped
2 stalks celery, diced
3 c. water
3 cubes beef bouillon
1/2 t. dried basil
1/2 t. dried oregano
1/2 t. salt
1/2 t. pepper
1-1/2 c. frozen mixed vegetables

Combine all ingredients except frozen vegetables in a 6-quart crockpot; mix gently. Cover and cook on high setting for 5 to 6 hours. Stir in frozen vegetables; cook for one additional hour. Makes 8 to 10 servings.

Browning isn't required for crockpot beef soups, but it does add a lot of flavor. Pat the beef cubes dry with a paper towel before browning... don't crowd the pieces in the pan, and be sure to stir up all the tasty browned bits at the bottom.

Tummy-Warming
SOUPS & BREADS

Vegetable Chowder

Bethi Hendrickson
Danville, PA

A quick and yummy meatless chowder that's tummy-warming on those chilly days.

3 T. butter
3 carrots, peeled and finely chopped
3/4 c. sweet onion, finely chopped
4 c. chicken broth
2 T. fresh parsley, finely chopped
1/2 t. salt
1/2 t. pepper
2 to 3 potatoes, peeled and diced
6 c. fresh or frozen corn
2 c. fat-free half-and-half
2 T. cornstarch
Garnish: shredded Cheddar cheese

Melt butter in a Dutch oven over medium heat. Add carrots and onion; sauté until onion is translucent. Add chicken broth, parsley, salt and pepper. Bring to a boil; add potatoes and corn. Combine half-and-half and cornstarch in a small bowl; mix well and stir into soup. Reduce heat to medium-low and simmer for 15 minutes, or until vegetables are tender. Serve in bowls, topped with cheese. Makes 8 servings.

Make your own freezer soup kits. Whenever you chop veggies and fresh herbs for soup, chop a little extra. Store in a freezer bag, ready to add to your next pot of soup...a great timesaver!

Super-Simple COMFORT FOODS

Famous Clam Chowder

Cathy Hillier
Salt Lake City, UT

A friend gave me this recipe from a long-ago restaurant here in Salt Lake City. We love it...please pass the saltines!

2 c. potatoes, peeled and diced
1 c. onions, diced
1 c. celery, diced
4 6-1/2 oz. cans chopped clams, drained and juice reserved
3/4 c. butter
3/4 c. all-purpose flour
4 c. half-and-half
1/2 t. sugar
1-1/2 t. salt
1/8 t. pepper

Combine all vegetables in a large saucepan. Add reserved clam juice and enough water to cover vegetables. Cover and simmer over medium-low heat for about 20 minutes; do not drain. Meanwhile, melt butter in a separate saucepan over low heat; stir in flour and half-and-half. Cook until thickened and smooth, stirring occasionally. Add flour mixture and clams to vegetable mixture. Stir in sugar, salt and pepper; heat through without boiling. Makes 8 servings.

New England Johnny Cakes

Julie Perkins
Anderson, IN

So good with ham & beans, chili or clam chowder!

1-1/2 c. all-purpose flour
3/4 c. yellow cornmeal
1/4 c. sugar
1 T. baking powder
1/2 t. salt
2 eggs, beaten
1 c. whipping cream

In a large bowl, sift together flour, cornmeal, sugar, baking powder and salt. Add eggs and cream; beat vigorously until smooth. Pour batter into a greased 9"x9" baking pan. Bake at 425 degrees for about 30 minutes. Cut into squares; serve warm. Serves 9.

A recipe is a story that ends with a good meal.
– Pat Conroy

Tummy-Warming SOUPS & BREADS

Mom's Go-To Potato Soup

Jodi Clardy
Haslet, TX

When time is tight or dinner plans go awry, this flavorful crockpot potato soup is my trusty go-to. A steaming bowl on a chilly day is pure comfort, and this recipe delivers all the warmth and flavor without the hassle of peeling and chopping potatoes.

30-oz. pkg. frozen shredded hashbrowns
10-3/4 oz. can cream of potato soup
1/2 c. onion, chopped
5-1/4 c. chicken broth
salt and pepper to taste
8-oz. pkg. cream cheese, cubed
Garnish: shredded Cheddar cheese, crumbled bacon, chopped green onions

In a 6-quart crockpot, combine all ingredients except cream cheese and garnish; mix gently. Cover and cook on low setting for 6 to 8 hours. About one hour before serving, add cream cheese. Cover and continue cooking until cream cheese has completely melted. Stir well. Serve with toppings of your choice. Makes 8 servings.

Creamy Mushroom Soup

Laura Fuller
Fort Wayne, IN

So creamy and comforting! We love this with crisp buttered toast.

1/4 c. butter
2 c. mushrooms, chopped
1/4 c. yellow onion, chopped
2 T. all-purpose flour
14-1/2 oz. can chicken broth
1 c. half-and-half
salt and pepper to taste

Melt butter in a large saucepan over medium-high heat. Sauté mushrooms and onion for 5 minutes, or until soft. Stir in flour until smooth; gradually stir in chicken broth. Cook and stir for 5 minutes, or until thick and bubbly. Stir in half-and-half; season with salt and pepper. Heat through, but do not boil. Serves 4.

Copycat Cheeseburger Soup

Hannah Stoltzfus
Denver, PA

When we lived in Lancaster County, Pennsylvania, we had so many Amish restaurants nearby. Katie's Kitchen was one of our favorites and most often visited by our out-of-town friends. Our meals there always included a cup of their cheeseburger soup, so I've loved making this at home!

1/2 lb. ground beef
1/4 c. butter
3/4 c. onions, chopped
3/4 c. carrots, peeled and grated
3/4 c. celery, diced
1 t. dried basil
1 t. dried parsley
3 c. chicken broth
3 c. potatoes, peeled and diced
1-3/4 c. milk
1/4 c. all-purpose flour
1/2 t. celery salt
1/2 t. salt
1/4 t. pepper
8-oz. pkg. shredded Cheddar cheese

Brown and crumble beef in a large soup pot over medium heat; drain. Add butter, onions, carrots, celery, basil and parsley; sauté for 5 to 6 minutes. Add chicken broth and potatoes; simmer until vegetables are tender. In a bowl, mix together milk, flour and seasonings; add to soup. Cook and stir until thickened; stir in cheese and simmer until cheese is melted. Makes 6 servings.

Watch tag sales for a big red speckled enamelware stockpot...it's just the right size for cooking up a family-size batch of soup. The bright color adds a homey touch to any soup supper!

Tummy-Warming SOUPS & BREADS

Chicken & Gnocchi Soup

Bethi Hendrickson
Danville, PA

When you're so hungry for this soup during a pandemic... what do you do? You make your own!

5 t. butter
2 T. olive oil
2 carrots, peeled and thinly sliced
1/4 c. onion, finely diced
2 cloves garlic, minced finely
1/4 c. all-purpose flour
2 c. chicken broth, divided
4 c. fat-free half-and-half
1 c. fresh spinach, chopped
2 c. chicken, cooked and shredded
1-1/2 14-1/2-oz. pkgs. refrigerated gnocchi pasta, uncooked
8-oz. pkg. finely shredded Parmesan cheese

In a large Dutch oven over medium heat, melt butter with olive oil. Sauté carrots, onion and garlic until onion is translucent. Sprinkle flour over vegetables. Increase heat to medium-high and cook for one minute, stirring constantly. Add 1/2 cup broth; cook and stir until well mixed. Reduce heat to medium-low; stir in remaining broth, half-and-half, spinach and chicken. Simmer for 10 to 15 minutes. Meanwhile, in a separate saucepan, cook gnocchi according to package directions. Drain and add to soup; stir in cheese. Simmer for about 5 minutes and serve. Makes 8 to 10 servings.

Whenever you finish a chunk of fresh Parmesan cheese, don't toss the rind! Freeze or refrigerate it to add to a pot of Italian-style soup. It will add rich flavor as it melts into the soup.

Quick Mexican Posole

Donna Acierno
Broomfield, CO

Our family loves this traditional Mexican soup, so I created this quick version that we can enjoy anytime we like. It was an instant hit! It works even on a hot summer day. Only a few minutes to heat on the stove and it's ready. Add your favorite toppings...corn chips are good with this too.

15-1/2 oz. can white or yellow hominy, drained
15-oz. can green chile sauce with chicken
10-3/4 oz. can cream of chicken soup
4-oz. can diced green chiles
1 to 2 c. cooked chicken, diced
1-1/4 c. milk or water
Optional: 1 to 2 T. jalapeño pepper, diced
Garnish: shredded Cheddar cheese, sour cream, chopped fresh cilantro or chives

In a large saucepan, combine all ingredients except optional garnish. Bring to a boil over medium-high heat. Reduce heat to low and simmer for 15 to 20 minutes, stirring occasionally. Serve with a little shredded cheese and other toppings, as desired. Serves 6.

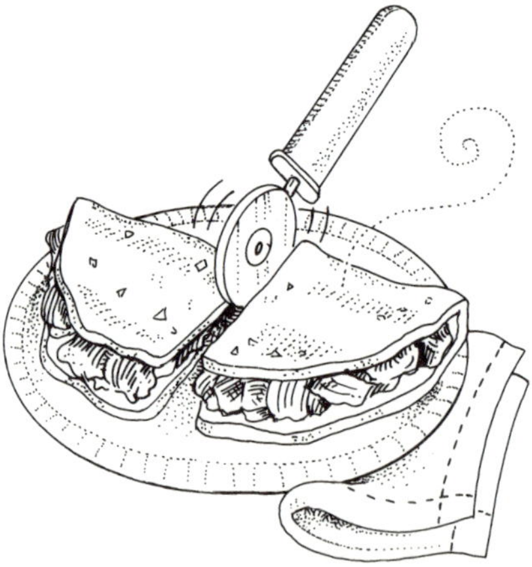

Cheesy quesadillas are quick and filling paired with soup. Sprinkle a flour tortilla with shredded cheese, top with another tortilla and toast lightly in a skillet until the cheese melts. Cut into wedges and serve with salsa.

Tummy-Warming SOUPS & BREADS

Zucchini & Sausage Soup

Sharon Theisen
St. Cloud, MN

A family favorite! Kids who don't like zucchini love this recipe and ask for more...they think they are eating potatoes!

1 lb. ground Italian pork sausage
2 c. celery, chopped
2-1/2 c. zucchini, peeled and cubed
1 c. onion, chopped
2 23-oz. cans diced tomatoes
1 t. Italian seasoning
1 t. dried oregano
1/2 t. dried basil
1/4 t. garlic powder
2 t. salt
1 t. sugar
2 green peppers, diced

Brown sausage in a soup pot over medium heat; drain. Add celery; cook for 10 minutes. Add remaining ingredients except green peppers; simmer for 20 minutes, stirring occasionally. Add green peppers and cook for 10 minutes. Makes 6 to 8 servings.

Sweet Potato Biscuits

Tina Matie
Alma, GA

These tasty biscuits have been a favorite in our home for years. They are very simple to make and a wonderful addition to any meal.

2 c. all-purpose flour
1 T. baking powder
1/2 t. salt
1/4 c. butter
1-1/2 c. cooked sweet potatoes, mashed
Optional: small amount milk

In a bowl, mix together flour, baking powder and salt. Cut in butter with a fork until mixture resembles coarse crumbs. Stir in mashed sweet potatoes. If the dough is too dry to hold together, add a little milk. Form dough into a ball and turn out onto a floured surface. Pat out dough to 1/2 inch-thick; cut with a biscuit cutter. Arrange on a greased baking sheet. Bake at 425 degrees for about 10 minutes, until very lightly golden. Makes about one dozen.

Easy Camp Stew

Amy Riley
Abbeville, AL

This recipe is a great find! It's easy to put together and inexpensive to keep the ingredients on hand. A side of easy cornbread mix baked while this stew is warming makes a delicious complement.

2 10-oz. cans chicken breast
5-oz. can smoked ham
14-3/4 oz. can creamed corn
14-1/2 oz. can petite diced tomatoes
15-oz. can corn, drained
15-oz. can diced potatoes, drained
14-1/2 oz. can lima beans, drained
1/3 c. barbecue sauce
2 T. Worcestershire sauce

Combine all ingredients in a Dutch oven; mix until well combined. Cook over medium heat-high heat, stirring occasionally, until stew starts to boil around the edges. Reduce heat to medium-low; simmer for 15 to 20 minutes and serve. Makes 6 servings.

Keep a notepad on the fridge to make a note whenever a pantry staple is used up...you'll never run out of that one item you need for dinner.

Tummy-Warming SOUPS & BREADS

Chili Cornbread

Beverly Verdery
Normal, IL

A delicious down-home savory cornbread you're sure to love.

2 eggs, beaten
1 c. yellow cornmeal
1 t. baking powder
1/2 t. baking soda
1/2 t. salt
2 T. butter, melted
1/2 c. onion, chopped
14-3/4 oz. can cream-style corn, drained
4-oz. can chopped green chiles, drained
1 c. shredded Cheddar cheese

In a large bowl, combine all ingredients except cheese; mix well. Pour half of batter into a greased 9" cast-iron skillet or round baking pan; sprinkle cheese in the center. Pour remaining batter over cheese. Bake at 350 degrees for 35 to 40 minutes, until set and golden. Cool slightly; cut into wedges. Makes 6 to 8 servings.

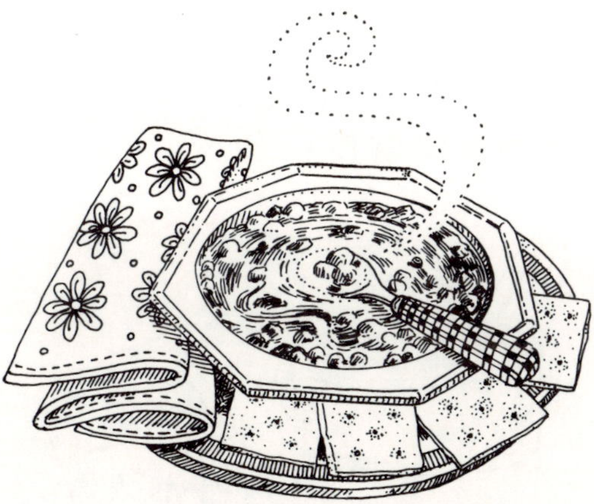

Soup tastes even better when refrigerated overnight before serving. As a bonus, you'll be able to lift off any fat that has solidified on the top.

White Chicken Chili

Katie Bonomo
Danville, IL

Deli rotisserie chicken and seasoning mix packets make this recipe super-easy! We love to top ours with mozzarella cheese...yum. So good on a cold night with some hot, homemade cornbread!

2 T. butter
1 c. onion, chopped
4 cloves garlic, minced
4-oz. can diced green chiles
3 to 4 c. cooked chicken, diced or shredded
2 15-1/2 oz. cans Great Northern beans
2 15-1/2 oz. cans cannellini beans
2 1-1/4 oz. pkgs. white chicken chili seasoning mix
Optional: 1 to 2 14-oz. cans chicken broth
Garnish: shredded mozzarella cheese

Melt butter in a large soup pot over medium heat; sauté onion and garlic until onion is translucent. Add chiles and sauté for about 5 more minutes. Add chicken, undrained beans and seasoning mixes; bring to a boil. Reduce heat to medium-low. Simmer for at least one hour, stirring occasionally. For a thicker soup, before serving, remove 2 cups of soup, blend with an immersion blender and return to soup pot. For a thinner soup, stir in chicken broth to desired consistency. Serve topped with mozzarella cheese. Makes 10 to 12 servings.

Thicken a pot of chili and add scrumptious corn flavor too. Combine 1/2 cup water and 1/4 cup masa harina flour (from the Mexican food aisle). Add to a simmering pot of chili, stir until smooth and cook until warmed through.

Tummy-Warming SOUPS & BREADS

Creamy Tomato-Basil Soup

Susan Roark
Abingdon, VA

When I was teaching school, we teachers all shared recipes. Recently I found this gem I'd tucked away. I have no idea where it came from, but it sure is good. Serve with buttered crusty bread or a good old grilled cheese sandwich.

2 10-3/4 oz. cans tomato soup
2-1/2 c. whole milk
1 c. whipping cream
14-1/2 oz. can petite diced tomatoes
1 t. fresh basil, finely chopped
1/2 t. salt
1/4 t. pepper

In a large saucepan over medium heat, whisk together tomato soup, milk and cream until smooth and free of lumps. Stir in tomatoes with juice, basil, salt and pepper. Bring to a simmer, but do not boil. Simmer over low heat for at least 40 minutes and serve. Makes 6 to 8 servings.

Easy Cheesy Muffins

Samantha Starks
Madison, WI

Simple to make...delicious with a bowl of hot soup.

1-1/2 c. all-purpose flour
1-1/2 T. sugar
1 t. baking powder
3 c. shredded Colby Jack cheese
1 egg, beaten
1 c. milk
1/4 c. butter, melted

In a large bowl, whisk together flour, sugar and baking powder; stir in cheese and set aside. In a separate bowl, whisk together egg, milk and butter until well mixed. Add egg mixture to flour mixture; stir well. Spoon batter into 12 greased muffin cups, filling 2/3 full. Bake at 375 degrees for 20 to 25 minutes. Makes one dozen.

For the tenderest muffins, stir batter just until moistened... a few lumps won't matter!

That Bean Soup That Everyone Likes

Kristyn Hall
Richmond, MI

This recipe was taken from multiple bean soup recipes, all of which I enjoyed. I added and subtracted ingredients until all six of my kids liked it. Now it is a favorite cool-weather comfort meal at our house, served with crusty bread.

1/4 c. olive oil
1/2 lb. smoked pork sausage, diced
1 onion, diced
2 stalks celery, diced
2 carrots, peeled and diced
2 cloves garlic, minced
1/3 c. pearl barley, uncooked
15-1/2 oz. can pinto beans, drained and rinsed
15-1/2 oz. can black beans, drained and rinsed
15-1/2 oz. can white beans, drained and rinsed
1/4 c. fresh parsley, minced
salt and pepper to taste

Heat olive oil in a large soup pot over medium heat. Sauté sausage, vegetables and barley until sausage is browned and onion is tender. Add enough water to cover ingredients by one inch; bring to a boil. Reduce heat to medium-low; cover and simmer for 45 minutes, stirring occasionally. Stir in all beans and continue simmering another 15 minutes. Stir in a little more water, if needed. Stir in parsley; season with salt and pepper. Makes 6 to 8 servings.

When a recipe calls for canned vegetables like tomatoes, green beans and corn, look for varieties with the seasonings already mixed in. You'll have fewer ingredients for you to buy and measure!

Tummy-Warming SOUPS & BREADS

Appalachian Wild Rice Soup

Tina Goodpasture
Meadowview, VA

This easy soup is delicious hot or cold...I can't seem to get enough of it! It's one of my favorite soups, especially with cornbread or crackers. The flavor gets better after it is reheated.

6.2-oz. pkg. fast-cooking long-grain & wild rice mix
4 c. 2% milk
10-3/4 oz. can cream of potato soup
8-oz. pkg. pasteurized process cheese, cubed
1/2 lb. sliced bacon
Optional: minced fresh chives or chopped green onions

In a large saucepan, prepare rice mix according to package instructions. Stir in milk, soup and cheese; cook and stir until cheese is melted. Meanwhile, cook bacon in a skillet over medium heat until crisp; drain well. Garnish soup with crumbled bacon and, chives or onions, if desired. Makes 6 to 8 servings.

Broccoli-Cheese Soup

Vivian Marshall
Columbus, OH

This rich, tasty soup is so good, served with a crisp tossed salad and warm Texas toast.

2 10-3/4 oz. cans Cheddar cheese soup
14-1/2 oz. can chicken broth
1-1/4 c. milk
32-oz. pkg. pasteurized process cheese, cubed
16-oz. pkg. frozen chopped broccoli
1/4 c. onion, chopped
salt and pepper to taste

Combine all ingredients in a large stockpot over low heat, cutting up any larger pieces of broccoli. Cook over low heat, stirring often, until cheese is melted. Continue to cook over low heat until soup thickens and is heated through. If it gets too thick, add a bit more milk, a little at a time. Makes 5 to 6 servings.

The greatest sweetener of human life is friendship.
– Joseph Addison

Vegetable Curry Stew

Jill Ball
Highland, UT

Nothing is more comforting on a cold dark night than a bowl of savory stew. It warms you from head to toe!

1-1/2 t. olive oil
3 carrots, peeled and chopped
1 onion, chopped
1 c. cauliflower, cut into bite-size flowerets
1/2 c. apple, peeled, cored and chopped
1-1/2 t. curry powder
1/8 t. coriander
1 T. all-purpose flour
2 c. chicken or vegetable broth, divided
1 russet potato, peeled and chopped
3/4 t. salt

Heat oil in a heavy soup pot over medium heat; add carrots, onion, cauliflower and apple. Cover and cook for about 10 minutes, until onion is soft but not golden. Mix in spices and cook for 2 more minutes. Remove one cup of soup mixture to a blender; add flour and one cup broth. Process until smooth; return to soup pot along with remaining broth. Bring to a boil. Reduce heat to medium-low; add potato and salt. Simmer for 15 minutes, stirring occasionally. Remove from heat and serve. Makes 4 servings.

For the best results when making soup, allow it to just simmer gently over low or medium-low heat. Giving it a stir now & then will prevent sticking to the pot.

Tummy-Warming SOUPS & BREADS

My Favorite Chili

Linda Thomas
Hamilton, OH

After several modifications to a co-worker's recipe, this is what Dad and I like best. We're not fond of spicy chili or other spicy foods...this hits the spot for us.

1-1/2 to 2 lbs. ground beef
3/4 c. onion, chopped
15-3/4 oz. can chili beans
12-oz. can tomato sauce
1 c. tomato juice
1 c. water
1-1/2 t. chili powder
1/2 t. seasoned salt
1/2 t. salt
1/4 t. pepper

Brown beef in a large skillet over medium heat; drain. Add remaining ingredients; bring to a boil. Reduce heat to medium low. Simmer for 30 to 60 minutes, stirring occasionally. Makes 6 to 8 servings.

Serve chili Cincinnati-style! For 2-way chili, ladle chili over a bowl of spaghetti. For 3-way, top chili and spaghetti with shredded cheese. For 4-way, spoon diced onions on top of the cheese...add chili beans to the stack for 5-way. Scrumptious!

Vegetable Beef & Barley Soup

Teresa Eller
Denham Springs, LA

This is one of my favorite ways to use leftovers after the holidays. When everyone is bored with the roast turkey and baked ham, this soup is a great change. If you prefer fresh veggies, just cut them up and toss them in. Instead of ground beef, you can use leftover roast beef...just cube it and add along with the onion.

10 c. water
6 cubes beef bouillon
3 T. Worcestershire sauce
1 t. smoke-flavored cooking sauce
2 c. quick-cooking barley, uncooked
1 lb. ground beef
1 onion, chopped
2 10-oz. pkgs. frozen mixed vegetables
salt and pepper to taste

In a large soup pot, combine water, bouillon and sauces. Bring to a boil over high heat; add barley. Meanwhile, in a skillet over medium heat, brown beef with onion. Drain; add to broth mixture along with vegetables. Reduce heat to medium-low. Simmer for 20 to 30 minutes, stirring occasionally, until vegetables are cooked to desired doneness. Season with salt and pepper as desired. Makes 4 to 6 servings.

Be a savvy shopper! Make a shopping list, grouping items by the area of the store where they're found. You'll breeze right down the aisles.

Tummy-Warming SOUPS & BREADS

Mom's Zucchini Soup

Paula Marchesi
Auburn, PA

This soup is so easy to make, I double the recipe. It's a delicious way to use up all that extra zucchini in the summertime.

2 c. zucchini, sliced
1/2 c. onion, chopped
1/2 c. carrot, peeled and chopped
1 T. butter
2 c. low-salt chicken broth
3/4 t. dried tarragon
salt and pepper to taste
1/2 t. garlic powder
2 c. milk
Garnish: paprika to taste

In a large saucepan over medium heat, sauté zucchini, onion and carrot in butter for 5 minutes. Add chicken broth and seasonings; bring to a boil. Reduce heat to medium-low. Cover and simmer for 15 to 20 minutes, until vegetables are tender. Working in batches, process soup to desired consistency in a blender or food processor; return to pan. Add milk; heat through without boiling. Garnish bowls of soup with a sprinkle of paprika. Makes 4 servings.

Butter Swim Biscuits

Kay Turner
Dothan, AL

These buttery biscuits are so tasty, and always come out well. I was never good at making biscuits until I made these. I promise you won't go wrong!

1/2 c. butter, sliced
2-1/2 c. all-purpose flour
2 c. buttermilk
4 t. baking powder
2 t. salt

Add butter to a microwave-safe 9"x9" glass baking pan; microwave until butter is melted. Mix remaining ingredients in a large bowl; dough will be thick and sticky. Pour dough into pan and spread it out to the sides of pan. Score dough into 9 to 12 equal squares; do not slice all the way through. Bake at 350 degrees for 25 to 30 minutes, until golden on top. Makes 9 to 12 biscuits.

Mushroom Tortellini Soup

Kathy Neuppert Swanson
Hemet, CA

Mushroom lovers rejoice...this recipe is for you! A savory, creamy delight awaits you. I put this recipe together to enjoy leftover ham and mushrooms. My husband and son loved this last-minute creation... me too! Especially good with warm rolls on the side.

1/2 c. butter
2 c. cooked ham, chopped
3 stalks celery, finely chopped
1 carrot, peeled and finely chopped
8-oz. container sliced mushrooms
2 10-1/2 oz. cans French onion soup
2 10-3/4 oz. cans cream of chicken soup
2 c. jarred Alfredo sauce
20-oz. pkg. refrigerated or frozen cheese tortellini, uncooked
salt and pepper to taste
Garnish: 4 to 6 slices bacon, crisply cooked and crumbled

Melt butter in a Dutch oven over medium heat. Add ham, celery, carrot and mushrooms; sauté for 2 to 3 minutes. Add soups and Alfredo sauce; stir gently until combined. Bring to a simmer; add tortellini and stir thoroughly. Cover and simmer gently for 10 minutes, or until tortellini is cooked through. Season with salt and pepper. Ladle into bowls; top each with crumbled bacon and serve. Makes 10 servings.

Need to add some zing to a pot of soup? Just add a splash of lemon juice or vinegar...a little salt & pepper might do the trick, too.

Tummy-Warming SOUPS & BREADS

Stuffed Pepper Soup

Jessica Kraus
Delaware, OH

Don't feel like stuffing peppers? Just toss it all together in a pot and serve with a big chunk of crusty bread!

1 lb. ground beef
1 green pepper, chopped
1/2 c. onion, diced
28-oz. can diced tomatoes
15-oz. can tomato sauce
14-1/2 oz. can beef broth
1 cube beef bouillon
2 T. brown sugar, packed
salt and pepper to taste
2 c. water
1 c. long-cooking rice, uncooked

Brown beef in a stockpot over medium heat; drain. Add green pepper and onion; cook for 5 minutes. Stir in tomatoes with juice, tomato sauce, beef broth, bouillon cube and brown sugar. Season with salt and pepper; bring to a boil. Reduce heat to low; cover and simmer for 40 minutes. Meanwhile, in a separate saucepan, bring water and rice to a boil over high heat. Reduce heat to medium-low; cover and simmer for 20 to 25 minutes, until rice is tender. Add cooked rice to soup and heat through. Makes 6 servings.

To get rid of that smell after slicing onions, simply hold your hands under cold running water along with a stainless steel spoon or other utensil.

Crockpot Cauliflower Cheese Soup

Beth Richter
Canby, MN

I love a comforting bowl of soup in the winter, but I'm allergic to broccoli, so I thought, let's try the next best thing. This soup is so good and so comforting! You'll want to make it again and again. If you can't find refrigerated diced potatoes, frozen southern-style hashbrowns work well too. Serve with crusty bread, or topped with croutons or French fried onions.

1 to 2 12-oz. pkgs. frozen cauliflower flowerets
20-oz. pkg. refrigerated diced potatoes
1 c. carrots, peeled and shredded
32-oz. pkg. pasteurized process cheese, cubed
32-oz. container chicken or vegetable broth
garlic salt and onion salt to taste

Add cauliflower, potatoes and carrots to a 6-quart crockpot. Place cheese chunks on top; pour broth over all. Cover and cook on low setting for 6 to 8 hours. Stir after 3 to 4 hours; add seasonings as desired. When done, serve as is, or for a smoother consistency, purée soup in crock with an immersion blender. Makes 6 to 8 servings.

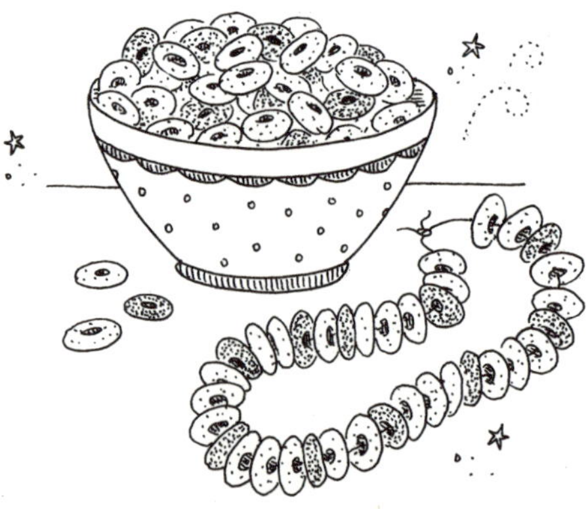

Set little ones down with a bowl of fruit-flavored cereal rings and a piece of dental floss...they can make cereal necklaces (and nibble away!) while you're getting dinner ready.

Tummy-Warming SOUPS & BREADS

Granny's Corned Beef & Tomato Soup

Mae Thurston
Haddock, GA

I grew up enjoying this soup that my granny made during the cold winter months. It was a budget-friendly way for her to feed a large family. Now I make it for my family and my granddaughter.

3 28-oz. cans whole tomatoes
4 to 6 potatoes, peeled and quartered
2 onions, each cut into 8 wedges
1-3/4 c. water
12-oz. can corned beef, flaked
salt and pepper to taste

Add tomatoes with juice to a large soup pot; use a spoon to crush tomatoes in pot. Add potatoes, onions and water; bring to a low boil over medium heat. Stir in corned beef; reduce heat to medium-low. Simmer for 30 minutes, or until potatoes are tender. Season with salt and pepper. Makes 8 servings.

Tina's Southern Cream Biscuits

Tina Goodpasture
Meadowview, VA

These are the easiest biscuits to make. I sometimes double the recipe for more biscuits...you can't eat just one!

2 c. self-rising flour
2 c. whipping cream

In a bowl, mix flour and cream until just blended. Drop dough by rounded teaspoonfuls onto a lightly greased 13"x9" baking pan. Bake at 450 degrees for 20 to 25 minutes, until lightly golden. Makes about one dozen.

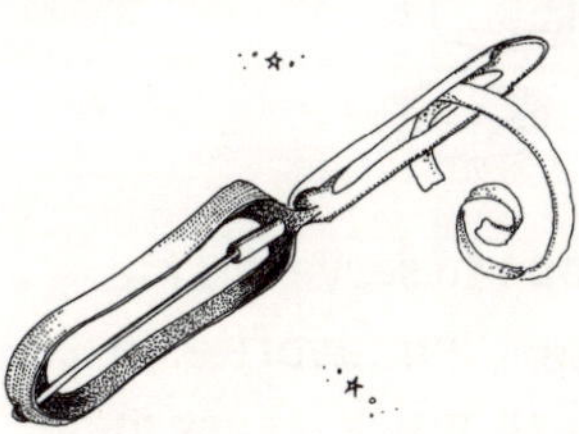

Use a potato peeler to quickly cut thin curls of cheese for garnishing soup, salad or pasta.

Crockpot Chicken Enchilada Soup

Emily Stuckey
Waynesville, NC

My husband and I love to make this tasty soup on the first chilly day every autumn. It is perfect for rainy weekends with a crackling fire and friends gathering to watch a football game.

3 boneless, skinless chicken breasts or thighs
16-oz. jar mild salsa verde or green enchilada sauce
14-1/2 oz. can chicken broth
1 c. water
8-oz. pkg. shredded taco-blend cheese
1/2 c. cream cheese, softened
1 c. whipping cream
3 6-inch flour tortillas, cut into bite-size pieces
Optional: 1 t. hot pepper sauce
Garnish: tortilla chips

Layer chicken pieces in a 6-quart crockpot; top with salsa, chicken broth and water. Cover and cook on low setting for 6 hours, or until chicken is very tender. Shred chicken in crock. Add cheeses, cream, tortilla pieces and hot sauce, if desired; stir. Cover and continue cooking on low setting for 30 minutes to one hour until cheese is melted, stirring a couple of times. Serve topped with tortilla chips. Makes 4 to 6 servings.

Freeze individual portions of leftover soup to serve later as a soup buffet supper...everyone can choose their favorite! Just add a basket of warm buttered rolls for a cozy, quick & easy meal.

Tummy-Warming SOUPS & BREADS

Chicken Noodle Soup

Emma Brown
Saskatchewan, Canada

Just like Mom used to make whenever one of us was feeling down. She'd add a handful of alphabet macaroni, just to cheer us.

2-1/2 c. wide egg noodles, uncooked
3 32-oz. containers low-sodium chicken broth
1 T. salt
1 t. poultry seasoning
1 c. celery, chopped
1 c. onions, chopped
1 c. carrots, peeled and chopped
1/3 c. cornstarch
1/4 c. water
3 c. cooked chicken, diced

Cook noodles according to package directions; drain. Meanwhile, in a large soup pot, combine chicken broth and seasonings. Bring to a boil over high heat. Stir in celery, onions and carrots. Reduce heat to medium; simmer for about 15 minutes, until vegetables are softened. In a small bowl, mix together cornstarch and water; gradually stir into soup. Fold in cooked noodles and chicken; heat through. Makes 10 to 12 servings.

Dilly Crackers

Erin Brock
Charleston, WV

Yummy for snacking...perfect with soup.

1 c. canola oil
1-oz. pkg. buttermilk ranch salad dressing mix
1 T. dried dill weed
1/2 t. garlic powder
16-oz. pkg. oyster crackers

Stir together oil, ranch dressing mix and seasonings in a large bowl. Add crackers and toss until evenly coated. Spread on an ungreased baking sheet. Bake at 200 degrees for 30 minutes, or until toasted and golden. Makes 15 to 20 servings.

Stir some alphabet macaroni into a pot of soup...the kids will love it!

Crockpot Italian Sausage & Orzo Soup

Michelle Tallman
Portland, OR

The ingredient list may look long, but this goes into the crockpot in a jiffy! I like to add a Parmesan rind for rich flavor. This would be nice made with tortellini as well. Serve with crusty Italian bread.

1 lb. ground sweet or spicy Italian pork sausage
14-1/2 oz. can crushed tomatoes
5 c. chicken or vegetable broth
15-oz. can cannellini or Great Northern beans, drained and rinsed
8-oz. can tomato sauce
3 carrots, peeled and diced
3 stalks celery, diced
1/2 onion, diced
2 cloves garlic, pressed
Italian seasoning, salt and pepper to taste
Optional: 1 Parmesan cheese rind
1 c. frozen cut green beans, thawed
1/2 c. orzo pasta, uncooked
Garnish: shredded Parmesan cheese

Brown sausage in a skillet over medium heat; drain. In a 6-quart crockpot, combine sausage, tomatoes with juice and remaining ingredients except green beans, pasta and cheese. Cover and cook on high setting for 4 hours. Add green beans; cover and cook another 30 minutes. Shortly before serving time, cook pasta according to package directions; drain. Remove Parmesan rind, if using. To serve, spoon some pasta into each bowl; ladle in soup. Top with cheese and serve. Makes 6 to 8 servings.

Soup is so nice when shared. Thank a friend with a basket of warm rolls and a pot of steaming homemade soup. What a welcome surprise on a brisk day!

SALADS
for Every Occasion

Mom-Mom's Simple Salad

Tracy Maurer
Gibbstown, NJ

This was my Mom-Mom's go-to salad in the summer whenever there were extra veggies to be used. Don't waste all those great farm favorites! The ingredients are easily increased to feed the number of people you're serving. Works great for spur-of-the-moment get-togethers or barbecues.

1 ripe tomato, sliced or cubed
1 cucumber, sliced or cubed
1 onion, sliced or cubed
1 pepper, any color, sliced or cubed

Combine all vegetables in a bowl; set aside. Pour Cider Vinegar Dressing over vegetables; mix gently. Cover and refrigerate for one to 2 hours, until serving time. Serve with a slotted spoon. Makes 4 servings.

Cider Vinegar Dressing:

1 c. sugar
1 c. cider vinegar
1 c. water

Combine all ingredients in a covered jar; add lid and shake until sugar dissolves.

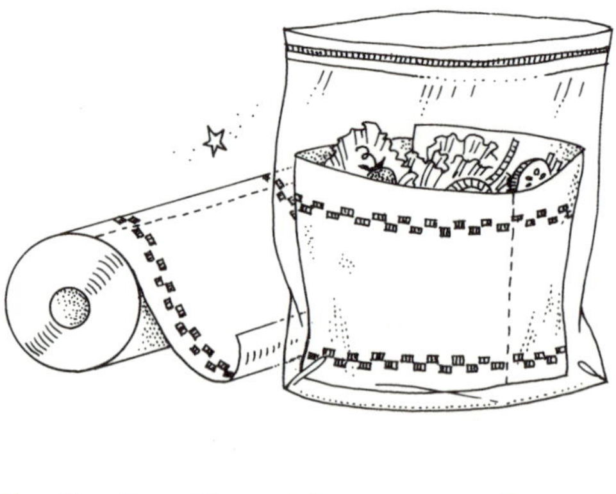

Keep vegetables fresh and nutritious! Wrap them in paper towels and refrigerate in unsealed plastic bags in the crisper drawer. Don't rinse veggies until you're ready to cook them.

SALADS
for Every Occasion

Macaroni Egg Salad

Crystal Shook
Catawba, NC

Great as a side with a sandwich, or as an appetizer served in individual mini canning jars for a party or shower.

16-oz. pkg. elbow macaroni, uncooked
4 eggs, hard-boiled and peeled
1 c. mayonnaise
3 T. mustard
1/4 c. dill pickles, chopped
salt and pepper to taste

Cook pasta according to package directions; drain. Rinse with cold water; drain and transfer to a large bowl. Chop eggs; add to bowl. Add remaining ingredients; gently fold together to blend well. Cover and refrigerate until chilled. Makes 8 to 10 servings.

Cranberry-Broccoli Slaw

Jill Steeley
Broken Arrow, OK

This salad is quick to fix, healthy and so tasty. It is my go-to salad recipe for potlucks.

12-oz. pkg. broccoli slaw
1 c. dried cranberries, chopped
1/2 c. sliced almonds
8-oz. bottle raspberry vinaigrette salad dressing

In a large bowl, combine broccoli slaw, cranberries and almonds; toss to mix. Cover and chill until serving time. Serve with raspberry vinaigrette on the side. Makes 6 to 8 servings.

Write "Tonight's Specials" with acrylic paint across the top of a small slate. Use chalk to update daily...let everyone know what's for dinner!

Carol's Potato Salad

Sandy Mendez
Phoenix, AZ

This delicious recipe was my godmother's, Carol Dennis. She was the best cook ever! This salad is still an all-time favorite. I was always asked to bring it for Thanksgiving and Christmas when we had dinner with my mother-in-law at her house every year. I don't use eggs in my salad, but add them if you like.

4 to 5 redskin potatoes
Optional: 2 eggs, hard-boiled, peeled and chopped
1/2 c. sweet pickle relish
1/4 c. onion, chopped
celery seed, salt and pepper to taste

Cover unpeeled potatoes with water in a saucepan; boil over high heat until tender. Drain and peel potatoes; chop and add to a large bowl. Add eggs, if using, and remaining ingredients. Mix gently. Stir in Pickle Relish Dressing. For best flavor, cover and refrigerate overnight before serving. Makes 6 to 8 servings.

Pickle Relish Dressing:

1 c. mayonnaise-style salad dressing
1/4 c. whipping cream or half-and-half
1/4 c. sweet pickle relish juice
1 t. mustard, or more to taste

Combine all ingredients; mix well.

Take time to share family stories and traditions with your kids! A cherished family recipe can be a great conversation starter at dinner.

SALADS
for Every Occasion

Delicious Spinach & Strawberry Salad

Sandra Paulin
Bloomington, IN

This fresh spinach salad reminds me of the arrival of spring. It's a favorite of our family.

1 lb. fresh strawberries, hulled and divided
6-oz. pkg. fresh spinach
1/2 cucumber, diced
2 T. onion, finely chopped
Optional: 1/4 c. sliced or slivered almonds

Prepare Strawberry Dressing, using 5 to 6 strawberries; slice remaining strawberries and set aside. Combine spinach, cucumber and onion in a large bowl; drizzle with dressing. Add sliced strawberries to salad; top with almonds, if desired. Serve immediately, or cover and refrigerate until ready to serve. Makes 6 servings.

Strawberry Dressing:

1 T. lemon juice
1 T. olive oil
1 T. sugar
5 to 6 strawberries

Mix together lemon juice, olive oil and sugar. Mash strawberries; stir into dressing.

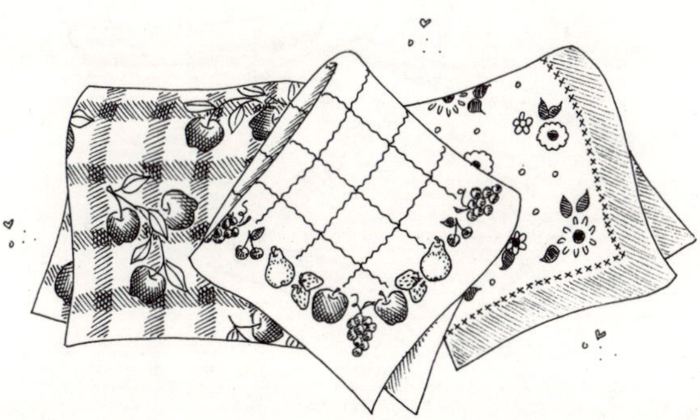

Colorful linen tea towels are a must for drying just-rinsed garden vegetables. They're reusable too...much less wasteful than paper towels!

Laura Ann's Tuna Macaroni Salad

Lisa Ann Panzino DiNunzio
Vineland, NJ

I can't even tell you how many pounds of this macaroni salad my sister has made throughout the years. People who were hesitant to try it with tuna ended up loving it, and would wait in anticipation for the next get-together for my sister to bring it again!

16-oz. pkg. elbow macaroni, uncooked
2 c. mayonnaise
1/4 c. celery, diced
1/4 c. onion, diced
2 5-oz. cans white albacore tuna in water, drained
salt and pepper to taste
Garnish: paprika

Cook macaroni according to package directions; drain. Rinse with cold water; drain and transfer to a large bowl. Add remaining ingredients except garnish; gently stir together until well blended. Cover and refrigerate for 3 to 4 hours, or overnight. At serving time, stir in additional mayonnaise if desired; garnish with paprika. Makes 10 servings.

Protect your favorite cookbook from cooking spatters... simply slip it inside a gallon-size plastic zipping bag.

SALADS
for Every Occasion

Simple Classic Coleslaw

Julie Warren
Lake Park, GA

I really love coleslaw, but not all restaurants have good slaw. I came up with this variation based on other recipes I'd seen. Now I can enjoy it at home anytime.

8-oz. pkg. tri-colored shredded coleslaw mix
2 T. plus 1 t. sweet pickle relish
1/3 c. olive oil mayonnaise
3 T. milk
salt and pepper to taste

Combine coleslaw and pickle relish in a large bowl; mix well and set aside. In a small bowl, whisk together mayonnaise and milk until creamy, similar to a salad dressing consistency. Add to slaw mixture and toss to mix well; season with salt and pepper. Cover and refrigerate until ready to serve. Makes 4 to 6 servings.

Creamy Cucumber Salad

Mary Warren
Sanford, MI

My German grandmother and my mom used to make this salad, and now my daughter also makes it. Good with any lunch or dinner. It's always a party or gathering favorite!

1 c. sour cream
1 T. vinegar
1 t. sugar
1/2 t. salt
1/8 t. pepper
3 c. cucumbers, thinly sliced
1/4 c. sweet onion, thinly sliced

Whisk together sour cream, vinegar, sugar, salt and pepper in a large glass bowl. Fold in cucumbers and onion. Cover and chill until serving time. Serves 6.

Keep sour cream fresh longer...store the tightly sealed container upside-down in the fridge.

Ramen Noodle Salad

Jeana Owens
Cumberland Gap, TN

This recipe is requested time & time again when we get together at our family reunion. My cousin tells me I should make three times as much as I do! They all enjoy it and it goes quickly. This can be made the day before serving.

2 3-oz. pkgs. chicken-flavored ramen noodles, divided
2 10-oz. pkgs. angel hair cabbage slaw, or 7 c. shredded cabbage
2 c. broccoli, chopped
1 c. slivered almonds
1 c. sunflower seeds
1 bunch green onions, chopped

Break ramen noodles into pieces; set aside seasoning packets from noodles. Combine noodles and remaining ingredients in a large bowl; toss well. At serving time, sprinkle reserved seasoning over salad, adding it to taste; pour Dressing over all and toss to mix. Makes 10 to 12 servings.

Dressing:

1 c. canola oil
1/3 c. white or cider vinegar
1/2 c. sugar

Whisk together all ingredients.

When you're shopping, let the kids pick out a new-to-them vegetable and help prepare it. Even picky eaters may be willing to try their very own veggie!

SALADS
for Every Occasion

Broccoli Salad Parisienne

Pamela Seely
Schaumburg, IL

A very easy, refreshing salad that's welcome in summertime or year 'round.

1/3 c. canola oil
1/4 c. vinegar
1 T. mustard
dried parsley and garlic powder to taste
1 t. salt
1/2 t. pepper
1 bunch broccoli, cut into bite-size flowerets

In a large bowl, whisk together all ingredients except broccoli. Add broccoli and toss to coat. Cover and chill at least one hour before serving. Toss again when ready to serve. Makes 6 to 8 servings.

Asian Chicken Slaw

Paula Marchesi
Auburn, PA

This is so easy and it has only five ingredients. I knew it was a winner the first time I served it...the bowl came back scraped clean!

3-oz. pkg. ramen noodles, divided
3-lb. deli rotisserie chicken
16-oz. pkg. shredded coleslaw mix
6 green onions, finely chopped
1 c. Asian toasted sesame seed salad dressing

Break ramen noodles into small pieces and add to a large bowl. (Reserve seasoning packet for another recipe.) Shred chicken, discarding skin and bones; add to bowl along with coleslaw mix and onions. Drizzle with salad dressing; toss to coat and serve. Makes 8 servings.

Add leftover herbs like basil, oregano and chives to your next summer salad for a pop of fresh flavor.

Black & White Bean Salad

Jackie Smulski
Lyons, IL

A picnic or party-pleaser salad! The bright citrus lime dressing adds a southwest taste. It contains no mayonnaise, so you don't have to worry about keeping it chilled. It can also be made a day ahead, as it's easy to prepare.

15-oz. can black beans, drained and rinsed
15-oz. can cannellini beans, drained and rinsed
1/2 red pepper, chopped
3 T. shallots or yellow onion, chopped
3 T. fresh cilantro, chopped

In a large bowl, combine all beans, red pepper, shallot or onion and cilantro; set aside. Drizzle with Dressing; toss to coat well. Cover and refrigerate until serving time. Makes 4 to 6 servings.

Citrus Lime Dressing:

5 T. olive oil
3 T. lime juice
3/4 t. paprika
3/4 t. salt
1/4 t. pepper

Whisk together all ingredients.

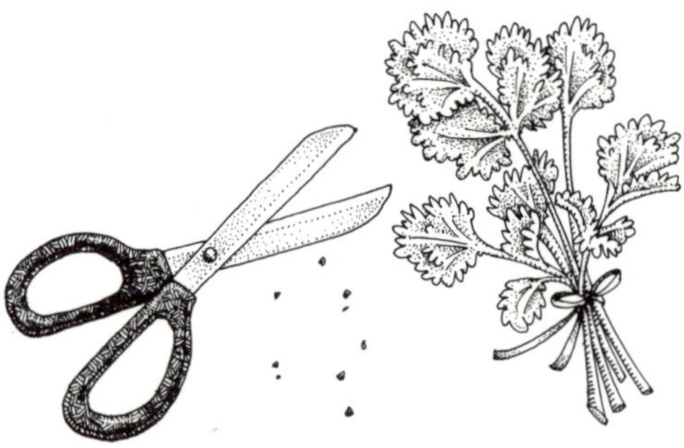

If you love south-of-the-border dishes but cilantro isn't to your taste, just replace it with parsley.

SALADS
for Every Occasion

Pretty Pea Salad

Janis Parr
Ontario, Canada

This pretty green pea salad is crunchy and very delicious! I came up with this recipe using some of my favorite ingredients.

2 c. frozen green peas
5 slices bacon, crisply cooked and coarsely crumbled
6-oz. can sliced water chestnuts, drained
1 c. celery, chopped
3 green onions, chopped
3/4 c. unsalted peanuts
2 T. chow mein noodles

Make Zesty Dressing ahead of time; chill. Close to serving time, combine frozen peas and remaining ingredients except chow mein noodles in a large bowl. Add the chilled dressing, gently stirring to combine. Sprinkle chow mein noodles over salad and serve. Makes 6 to 8 servings.

Zesty Dressing:

1/2 c. mayonnaise
1/4 c. Italian salad dressing

Stir together mayonnaise and salad dressing well. Cover and chill.

Pick up a bunch of fresh flowers when you shop for groceries. Tucked into a pitcher or glass jar, even simple daisies are charming and cheerful!

Derby City Chicken Salad

Ronda Hauss
Bluffton, SC

My family loves chicken salad, so I decided to add a special ingredient...ground ginger. Everyone who tries my version always asks for the recipe. It's wonderful to make when it's too hot to cook in the kitchen. I simply cook the chicken breasts in an electric steamer outside so the kitchen stays cool. This is especially handy when we spend the weekend at the lake! Greek yogurt may be used for some of the mayonnaise.

3/4 c. reduced-fat mayonnaise
1/2 t. ground ginger
1/2 t. salt
3 c. cooked boneless, skinless chicken breasts, cubed
1-1/2 c. red seedless grapes, cut in half
2/3 c. celery, sliced
1/2 c. green onions, sliced
Optional: 1/2 c. walnut pieces
Garnish: lettuce leaves, toasted bread or crackers

In a large bowl, combine mayonnaise, ginger and salt. Fold in chicken, grapes, celery, green onions and walnuts, if using. Cover and chill at least 2 hours or overnight. Serve on lettuce leaves, slices of toasted bread or crackers. Makes 6 to 8 servings.

Mix up a zesty salad dressing in an almost-empty Dijon mustard jar! Add 3 tablespoons olive oil, 2 tablespoons cider vinegar and a minced garlic clove to the jar. Replace the lid and shake well; season with salt, pepper and chopped fresh herbs, if you like.

SALADS
for Every Occasion

Everyday Go-To Spinach Salad

Donna Carter
Ontario, Canada

A friend of mine makes this salad all the time. It's time-saving, easy to prepare and so delicious. Now it is my go-to everyday salad, too. Can be made the day before. The cherry tomatoes are optional, but add a dash of color.

6-oz. pkg. fresh baby spinach
8-oz. pkg. sliced mushrooms
1 red onion, thinly sliced
Optional: 4 to 5 cherry tomatoes, cut in half
8-oz. bottle raspberry vinaigrette salad dressing

In a large bowl, combine all ingredients except salad dressing; mix well. Cover and refrigerate until ready to serve. Add dressing just before serving, using just enough dressing to coat. Serves 6 to 8.

Quickie Lettuce Salad

Pam Hooley
LaGrange, IN

Sometimes the simpler, the better! This is my aunt's recipe that I have used to round out more than one meal in my time.

4 eggs, hard-boiled, peeled and diced
1 head lettuce, chopped
1/2 c. real bacon bits

Combine eggs, lettuce and bacon bits in a large bowl; toss to mix and set aside. Just before serving, spoon Dressing over salad and stir. Makes 6 to 8 servings.

Dressing:

1 c. mayonnaise-style salad dressing
1/2 c. sugar
2 T. vinegar

Whisk together all ingredients until sugar dissolves.

Cranberry Fluff Salad

Wendy Ball
Battle Creek, MI

This was one of my Grandma Lockway's favorite salads to serve at our holiday tables. It's a recipe that's been around for a long time, at least as far back as I can remember (and I'm in my 60s!) and before frozen whipped topping was invented. Grandma used whipped cream in it. Now this is something that my grandchildren can help make, just like I helped my grandmother. If you can find the rainbow marshmallows, it's even more fun.

2 c. fresh cranberries
3/4 c. mini marshmallows
3/4 c. sugar
1/2 c. Honey Crisp, Fuji or Braeburn apple, cored and diced
1/2 to 3/4 c. canned pineapple, diced and drained
1/2 c. seedless green or red grapes
1/2 c. chopped pecans or walnuts
1/4 t. salt
2 c. frozen whipped topping, thawed

Grind cranberries in a food processor or food grinder. Transfer to a large bowl; add marshmallows and sugar. Cover and refrigerate overnight. On serving day, add apples, pineapple, grapes, nuts and salt; fold in whipped topping. Transfer to a pretty serving bowl; cover and chill until ready to serve. Makes 8 to 10 servings.

A happy family is but an earlier heaven.
– Sir John Bowring

SALADS
for Every Occasion

Frozen Fruit Salad

Tina Goodpasture
Meadowview, VA

I love this salad...it's colorful and easy to make. I like the fruit in it, too! I usually freeze it for a day for the flavors to mix together.

14-oz. can sweetened condensed milk
8-oz. container frozen whipped topping, thawed
2 c. mini marshmallows
1 c. shredded coconut
21-oz. can cherry pie filling
20-oz. can crushed pineapple, drained
2 11-oz. cans mandarin oranges, drained

Mix all ingredients together in a large bowl. Spoon into a 13"x9" glass baking pan; cover and freeze. Thaw slightly before serving; cut into squares. Makes 15 to 18 servings.

Caramel Apple Salad

Judy Taylor
Butler, MO

An old favorite! This variation of apple salad is easy to make and yummy to eat, especially in the autumn.

8-oz. container frozen whipped topping, thawed
3-1/2 oz. pkg. instant butterscotch pudding mix
8-oz. can crushed pineapple
1 c. mini marshmallows
1 c. dry-roasted peanuts
3 c. apples, cored and cubed

Combine whipped topping, dry pudding mix and remaining ingredients in a large bowl; mix well. Cover and chill. Serves 6 to 8.

For potlucks and picnics, serve up slaws and salads in colorful clear plastic cups...clean-up is a snap!

Mom's Macaroni Salad

Jan Purnell
Littlestown, PA

My mom used to make this salad with boiled dressing for every informal family gathering. It was the most-requested dish at larger gatherings as well, so she often doubled and tripled the recipe. It was always the first thing to go on any table on which it was presented. She would often slice extra hard-boiled eggs and arrange them on top, garnished with a sprinkling of paprika.

2 c. elbow macaroni, uncooked
3 eggs, hard-boiled, peeled and diced
1 c. mayonnaise
2 T. mustard
1 c. celery, chopped
1/2 c. onion, chopped

Prepare Boiled Dressing; allow to cool. Meanwhile, cook macaroni according to package directions; drain. Rinse with cold water; drain and add to a large bowl. Add remaining ingredients and dressing; mix well. Cover and chill overnight. Makes 9 servings.

Boiled Dressing:

1-1/2 c. water
1/2 c. vinegar
1/4 c. all-purpose flour
1-1/2 c. sugar
1-1/2 t. salt

Combine all ingredients in a saucepan over medium heat. Bring to a boil; boil for 5 minutes, stirring often. Cool.

Save that leftover pickle juice! It makes a tasty addition to potato and macaroni salads and deviled eggs.

Rice & Shrimp Salad

Janis Parr
Ontario, Canada

This simple and tasty recipe is a favorite and can be made ahead...so convenient. Salmon, tuna or ham can be substituted for the shrimp. A few sprigs of fresh parsley tucked in around the edges make it such a pretty dish for the buffet table.

1-1/2 c. tomato juice
1/2 t. salt
1-1/2 c. instant rice, uncooked
1/2 c. dill pickles, finely chopped and drained
1 T. onion, grated
1/4 t. pepper
2 c. cooked shrimp, cleaned and chopped
2/3 c. mayonnaise

In a saucepan over medium heat, combine tomato juice and salt; bring to a boil. Stir in rice; cover and set aside for 10 minutes, or until rice has absorbed all liquid. Add dill pickle, onion and pepper and stir well. Cover and chill. Shortly before serving, add shrimp and mayonnaise; stir to combine. Serve chilled. Makes 6 to 8 servings.

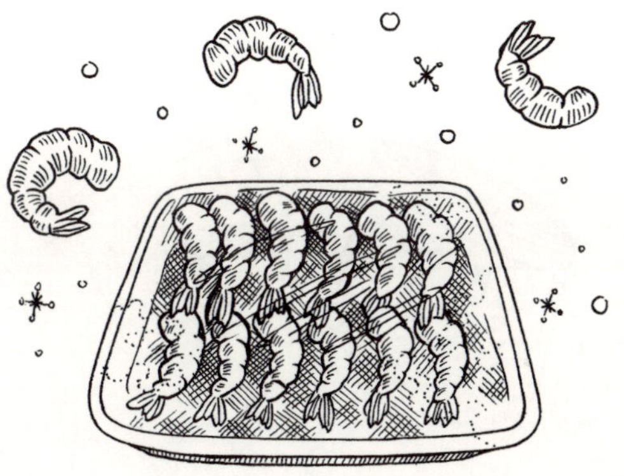

Keep frozen shrimp on hand for delicious meals anytime...let it thaw overnight in the fridge. Or, for a quicker way, place the frozen shrimp in a colander, run ice-cold water over it and drain well.

Greek Chickpea Salad

Julie Perkins
Anderson, IN

Simple, easy and delicious! Great on its own, or served as a side. Serve with Italian bread.

2-1/2 c. canned chickpeas, drained
1/2 sweet onion, sliced and separated into rings
1 ripe tomato, cut into chunks
1/2 t. salt
pepper to taste

Make Lemony Dressing; set aside. Combine chickpeas, onion and tomato in a large bowl. Toss with dressing; season with salt and pepper. Serve immediately, or cover and chill until serving time. Makes 6 to 8 servings.

Lemony Dressing:

2 T. olive oil
2 T. lemon juice
2 T. water
1 t. sugar

Whisk together all ingredients.

Hungry kids at home? Whenever you bring home groceries, label any packages of cheese, veggies and fruit that are fine for between-meal snacking. The ingredients for tomorrow's dinner won't turn into munchies!

SALADS
for Every Occasion

Summer Corn Salad

Delores Lakes
Mansfield, OH

Fresh sweet corn is the best! I look forward to using it in recipes all summer long. If you get hungry for this salad outside of corn season, you can use frozen corn as well. This can be put together quickly for an impromptu picnic or gathering.

2 c. fresh or frozen sweet corn
3/4 c. ripe tomato, chopped
1/2 c. red pepper, chopped
1/2 c. celery, chopped
1/4 c. red onion, chopped
1/4 c. ranch salad dressing
salt and pepper to taste
Optional: 1 T. sugar

Combine all vegetables in a large salad bowl; toss to mix. Stir in salad dressing, salt, pepper and sugar, if using. Cover and refrigerate until serving time. Makes 8 servings.

For speedy meal prep, set a bowl on your kitchen counter to collect scraps and trimmings while you cook. Then just make one trip to the trash can or compost bin when you're all done. Clever!

Tropical Rice Salad

Janis Parr
Ontario, Canada

The combination of flavors and textures in this salad makes it a true crowd-pleaser. You will be asked to share this recipe!

2-1/2 c. cooked rice
11-oz. can mandarin oranges, drained
8-oz. can whole water chestnuts, drained and sliced
1/2 c. celery, chopped
1/2 c. sliced mushrooms
1/2 c. chopped almonds
1/3 c. onions, finely chopped
2 T. fresh chives, chopped

Make Soy Dressing; set aside. Add cooked rice to a salad bowl. Drizzle dressing over rice, stirring well. Cover and chill for at least 4 hours. Stir in remaining ingredients. Serve chilled. Makes 6 to 8 servings.

Soy Dressing:

1/2 c. oil
1/2 c. white vinegar
2 T. soy sauce

Combine all ingredients in a jar; add lid and shake until well mixed.

Using recycled jars for salad dressings and sauces? Remove stubborn labels and inked expiration dates with a swab of rubbing alcohol.

SALADS
for Every Occasion

Auntie's Fruited Cheese Salad

Doreen Knapp
Stanfordville, NY

I found this recipe in my auntie's cookbook with a note that said, "From Gert". My aunt loved to swap recipes with her friends, as she was a Navy wife for over 20 years. So thank you, Gert. It's a delicious salad that I love to eat any time of day.

3 c. cottage cheese
2 16-oz. containers frozen whipped topping, thawed
6-oz. pkg. orange-pineapple gelatin mix
2 8-oz. cans pineapple tidbits, drained
11-oz. can mandarin oranges, drained

Combine cottage cheese and whipped topping in a large bowl; stir until well blended. Stir in dry gelatin mix; fold in pineapple and oranges. Press into an 8-cup gelatin mold, or spoon into a serving bowl. Cover and chill for several hours. Makes 8 to 10 servings.

One-Cup Salad

Betty Kozlowski
Newnan, GA

Some dear friends from Georgia gave me this recipe during my traveling years as a young single woman, many years ago.

5-oz. can evaporated milk
3-oz. pkg. orange gelatin mix
8-oz. can crushed pineapple, drained
1/2 c. mayonnaise
1 c. finely shredded sharp Cheddar cheese

Heat evaporated milk in a saucepan over low heat, being careful not to boil. Stir in gelatin mix until dissolved. Add remaining ingredients and blend well. Pour mixture into a serving bowl. Cover and refrigerate until set, at least 30 minutes. Serves 4 to 6.

Crunchy Strawberry Salad

Elizabeth Smithson
Mayfield, KY

This recipe has been in the family for years...it's my favorite go-to salad for a delicious treat. So good and refreshing!

3-oz. pkg. ramen noodles, divided
1 c. chopped walnuts
1/4 c. butter
8 c. romaine lettuce, torn
2 c. fresh strawberries, hulled and sliced
1/2 c. green onions, chopped

Prepare Dressing ahead of time; refrigerate. Break ramen noodles into small pieces. (Reserve seasoning packet for another recipe.) In a skillet over medium heat, sauté noodles and walnuts in butter until golden, stirring often. Cool on paper towels. At serving time, combine lettuce, strawberries and onions in a large bowl. Drizzle with dressing and toss to coat. Top with noodle mixture and serve. Makes 8 to 10 servings.

Dressing:

1/4 c. oil
1/4 c. sugar
2 T. rice vinegar
1/2 t. soy sauce

Mix all all ingredients in a jar; add lid and shake until sugar is dissolved.

Don't toss those leftover ramen seasoning packets! Just a sprinkle gives terrific flavor to cooked vegetables, soups and rice dishes.

SALADS
for Every Occasion

Carolina Coleslaw

Diana Krol
Hutchinson, KS

This is a great coleslaw recipe for summer picnics and barbecues. The sweet-and-sour flavor pairs perfectly with fried chicken and fish, hamburgers and hot dogs. Plus, it can be made a day ahead of time to serve chilled...very convenient!

1 head cabbage, shredded
1 red pepper, diced
1/4 c. onion, minced

Make Mustard Dressing; set aside. Stir together all vegetables in a large bowl. Pour hot dressing over vegetables and stir to mix well. Cover and chill for several hours or overnight. Serve chilled. Makes 6 to 8 servings.

Mustard Dressing:

1 c. sugar
1 t. dry mustard
1 t. celery seed
1 t. salt
1 c. vinegar
2/3 c. oil

In a small saucepan, combine sugar, mustard, celery seed and salt; stir in vinegar and oil. Bring mixture to a boil; cook and stir until sugar is dissolved.

Add mandarin oranges or pineapple tidbits to your favorite coleslaw for a fruity tropical accent that goes well with fish dishes.

Cafe Pasta Salad

Candace Middleton
Campton, KY

Family & friends always ask for this salad at potlucks. A great group of cafeteria cooks at a local hospital whip this together occasionally, and it always sells out. There was no recipe available, so I watched them prepare it and jotted down a version for home. You can add cherry tomatoes or red onion for a more colorful version.

16-oz. pkg. rotini pasta, uncooked
5 slices bacon, crisply cooked and crumbled
1 c. fresh broccoli, cut into bite-size pieces
1 c. fresh cauliflower, cut into bite-size pieces
1 c. shredded Cheddar cheese

Cook pasta according to package instructions; drain. Rinse with cold water; drain and add to a large bowl. Add remaining ingredients and Buttermilk Ranch Dressing; toss to mix well. Cover and chill; serve chilled. Makes 8 to 10 servings.

Buttermilk Ranch Dressing:

1 c. buttermilk
1 c. mayonnaise
1-oz. pkg. ranch salad dressing mix

Combine all ingredients; whisk together well.

Tuck packets of gravy and seasoning mix into a napkin holder to keep the pantry tidy.

SALADS
for Every Occasion

Veggie Chopped Salad

Judy Phelan
Macomb, IL

This is a recipe from my grandmother's recipe box. She loved her garden. You'll love this salad...it's fresh and easy to put together.

6 slices bacon, crisply cooked and crumbled
3 c. broccoli, chopped
3 c. cauliflower, chopped
3 c. celery, chopped
2 c. frozen peas, thawed
3/4 c. salted peanuts

Combine all ingredients except peanuts in a large bowl. Add Parmesan Dressing and toss to coat. Cover and chill until serving time. Stir in peanuts just before serving. Makes 10 to 12 servings.

Parmesan Dressing:

1-1/2 c. mayonnaise
1/4 c. sugar
2 T. grated Parmesan cheese
1 T. cider vinegar
1/4 t. salt

In a small bowl, mix together all ingredients.

For a speedy Greek salad, combine quartered roma tomatoes with sliced black olives, crumbled feta cheese and chopped red onion. Drizzle with Greek vinaigrette or Italian salad dressing and toss to mix.

Taco Pasta Salad

Tina Matie
Alma, GA

This salad is simple to make and so delicious! It's a big hit at my church's Fourth of July social gathering. Everyone loves it and the bowl is scraped clean. It has all the best parts of a taco, but served as a pasta salad instead and topped with crunchy tortilla chips. Yum!

3 c. rotini pasta, uncooked
1 lb. ground beef
1-oz. pkg. taco seasoning mix
1 lb. cherry tomatoes, cut in half
1 c. shredded Monterey Jack cheese
1 c. shredded Cheddar cheese
1 c. Catalina or French salad dressing
2 c. nacho cheese tortilla chips, crushed

Cook pasta according to package directions; drain. Rinse with cold water; drain well and set aside. Meanwhile, brown beef in a large skillet over medium heat, breaking it up into crumbles, until no pink is left; drain. Stir in taco seasoning; mix well and remove from heat. In a very large bowl, combine cooked pasta, beef mixture, cherry tomatoes, cheeses and salad dressing. Stir until combined and everything is coated in dressing. Cover and refrigerate for at least 4 hours. Just before serving, mix in crushed tortilla chips; serve immediately. Serves 10 to 12.

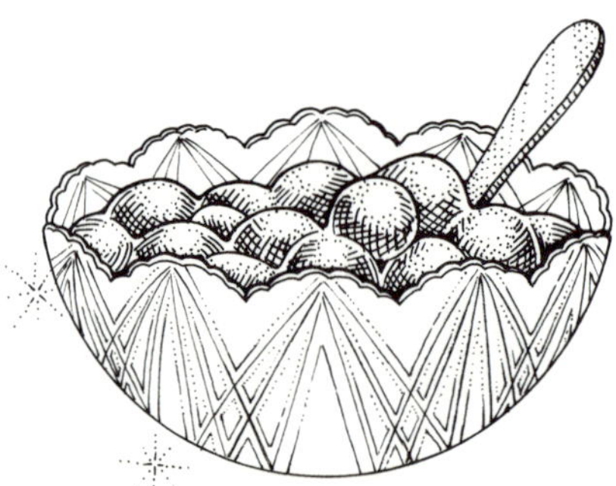

A large clear glass bowl is a must for serving family & friends. Serve up a layered salad, a fruity punch or a sweet dessert trifle. You'll wonder what you did without it!

Fresh & Tasty
SIDES

Scalloped Sweet Corn

Gladys Kielar
Whitehouse, OH

We enjoy summer corn in Ohio as corn on the cob and in casseroles, too. This recipe is extra tasty made with fresh-picked corn.

2 c. fresh or frozen corn
2 eggs, beaten
1 c. milk
2/3 c. saltine cracker crumbs
3 T. butter, melted
1 T. onion, minced
1 T. sugar
1/2 t. salt
1/4 t. pepper

Combine all ingredients in a large bowl and mix well. Spoon into a lightly greased 2-quart casserole dish. Bake, uncovered, at 350 degrees for 40 minutes, or until bubbly and golden. Makes 6 servings.

Set a regular dinner theme for each night of the week...Italian Night, Taco Night and Soup & Salad Night, based on your family's favorites. Meal planning will be a snap!

Fresh & Tasty SIDES

Laura's Creamy Potatoes

Leona Krivda
Belle Vernon, PA

My daughter Laura served these potatoes with a meal she made for us, and we loved them. They are so easy to make in a crockpot... and who doesn't like potatoes!

10-3/4 oz. can cream of chicken soup
2 c. sour cream
2 c. pasteurized process cheese, cubed
30-oz. pkg. frozen diced potatoes
1/2 onion, very finely chopped
1/4 t. salt, or to taste
1/4 t. pepper, or to taste

Spray a 4-quart crockpot with non-stick vegetable spray. Add all ingredients to crockpot; mix well. Cover and cook on low setting for 3 to 4 hours, until potatoes are tender and cooked through and cheese is melted. Makes 8 to 10 servings.

After you've unpacked groceries, take just a little time to prep ingredients and place them in plastic zipping bags...wash and chop fruits and vegetables and place meats in marinades. Weeknight dinners will be so much easier.

Rice & Mushroom Casserole

Lorraine Hollabaugh
Youngstown, OH

Great side dish! This recipe has been a favorite of mine since I was a kid. Mom always made us a favorite dish on our birthday, and this is the one I always chose. I believe the recipe came from the back of a soup can. More than 40 years later, it is still one of my favorite dishes and is now also one of my husband's favorites. We love it, especially on holidays. Hope you enjoy it too!

1 c. long-cooking rice, uncooked
10-1/2 oz. can French onion soup
10-1/2 oz. can beef broth
8-oz. can sliced mushrooms, drained and divided
1/2 c. butter

Spread uncooked rice in a greased 2-quart casserole dish. Add onion soup, beef broth and half of mushrooms; stir to mix well. Place butter on top, in the center. Cover and bake at 350 degrees for 30 minutes. Remove from oven; add remaining mushrooms and mix well. Bake, covered, for an additional 30 minutes, or until liquid is absorbed and rice is soft. Makes 6 to 8 servings.

Cloth napkins make mealtime just a little more special, with no paper napkins to throw away. Glue or stitch fun charms to napkin rings, so everyone can identify their own napkin easily.

Fresh & Tasty SIDES

Tina's Slow-Cooked Green Beans

Tina Goodpasture
Meadowview, VA

This recipe reminds me of my Granny's green beans. They are so tender and yummy! The house smells so good while this is cooking. I can make a meal on just green beans.

1 lb. fresh green beans, trimmed and broken in half
10-1/2 oz. can French onion soup
3/4 c. water
1/4 c. sliced pimentos, drained
1 T. olive oil
1 t. garlic, minced
1/2 t. pepper
1/4 c. toasted sliced almonds

In a 4-quart crockpot, combine all ingredients except almonds; stir well. Cover and cook on low setting for 4 hours, or on high setting for 2 hours. Sprinkle with almonds just before serving. Makes 6 to 8 servings.

Favorite Corn Casserole

Jane Ganey
Vandiver, AL

This is a family recipe that we always enjoy every year at Thanksgiving. It's scrumptious...people ask for it!

10-3/4 oz. can cream of celery soup
8-oz. container sour cream
3 11-oz. cans summer crisp corn, drained
8-oz. pkg. shredded Cheddar cheese
2 sleeves round buttery crackers, crushed
1/2 c. butter, melted

In a large bowl, stir together celery soup and sour cream; fold in corn. Transfer mixture to a greased 11"x8" baking pan. Sprinkle with shredded cheese; cover with crushed crackers and drizzle with butter. Bake, uncovered, at 350 degrees for 30 minutes. Makes 8 servings.

Dutch Crust Sweet Potato Casserole

Teresa Verell
Roanoke, VA

This recipe is a family favorite...it is is always requested for Thanksgiving dinner.

3 c. cooked sweet potatoes
1/2 c. plus 2-1/2 T. butter, melted and divided
1/2 c. evaporated milk
1/2 c. sugar
1 c. chopped walnuts
1/2 c. brown sugar, packed
1/4 c. all-purpose flour

Mash sweet potatoes in a large bowl. Add 1/2 cup melted butter, evaporated milk and sugar; mix well. Spoon into a buttered 2-quart casserole dish. Combine remaining butter, walnuts, brown sugar and flour; mix well and spoon over sweet potato mixture. Bake, uncovered, at 350 degrees for 25 minutes, until bubbly and golden. Makes 6 to 8 servings.

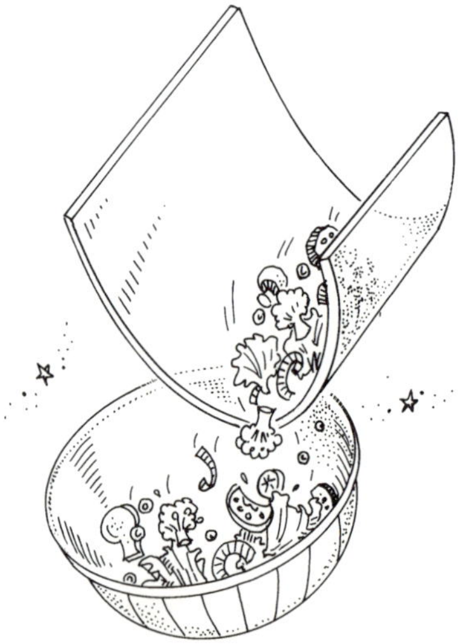

A flexible plastic cutting mat makes speedy work of slicing and dicing. Keep 2 mats on hand for chopping veggies and meats separately.

Fresh & Tasty SIDES

Mom's Homemade Applesauce

Rosemary Trezza
Winter Springs, FL

When we lived on Long Island, every year we went apple picking at a farm on the eastern part of Long Island. Our family was young and had so much fun seeing who could pick the most apples. We would bring my parents along with us also. Of course, after we returned home, the work began! But, the children couldn't wait until the homemade applesauce was ready. Many times, we enjoyed it warm instead of waiting for the applesauce to get cold in the fridge. Sweet memories!

8 Gala apples, peeled, cored and chopped
1/2 c. water
3/4 c. sugar

Add apples and water to a large saucepan over medium heat. Cook, stirring occasionally, until apples are nearly tender. Stir in sugar; cook for another 5 to 10 minutes. Transfer to a storage container; let cool. Cover and refrigerate or freeze. Recipe may be doubled. Makes 4 to 6 servings.

Keep apple pie spice on hand to use in all kinds of dishes... even sprinkle it into hot coffee and cider. A blend of cinnamon, nutmeg and allspice, it's like a whole spice rack in a little can.

Vicki's Zucchini Casserole

Vicki Van Donselaar
Cedar, IA

Fresh-from-the-garden vegetables and down-home bacon make this vegetable casserole so yummy!

2 c. zucchini, cubed
1/4 c. long-cooking rice, uncooked
2 ripe tomatoes, sliced
1 onion, sliced
1/2 t. dried oregano
pepper to taste
8-oz. pkg. pasteurized process cheese, sliced
6 to 8 slices bacon

In a greased 8"x8" baking pan, layer zucchini, uncooked rice, tomatoes and onion. Sprinkle with oregano and pepper. Layer with cheese slices and uncooked bacon slices. Bake, uncovered, at 350 degrees for one hour. Makes 8 to 10 servings.

Ann's Baked Potatoes

Patricia Thomas
Cataula, GA

My family has requested these potatoes every Thanksgiving and Christmas for 50 years...so you know they're good! Yukon Gold or redskin potatoes can also be used.

5 to 6 russet potatoes
1 to 2 T. olive oil, divided
salt and pepper to taste

Cut potatoes in half lengthwise. Cut each half into 2 to 4 equal pieces, depending on size of potatoes. Brush the bottom of a 13"x9" baking pan lightly with olive oil; arrange potatoes in pan. Spoon remaining oil over potatoes; season with salt and pepper. Bake, uncovered, at 350 degrees for 15 to 20 minutes. Spoon oil in pan over potatoes; bake another 15 minutes, or until tender and crusty. Makes 4 to 5 servings.

Fill the sink with hot soapy water when you start dinner and just toss in pans and utensils as they're used...clean-up will be a breeze.

Fresh & Tasty SIDES

Nana Hazel's Famous Broccoli & Rice Casserole

Hazel Umbehant
Cornelia, GA

Simple to make, and everyone loves this dish!

10-oz. pkg. frozen chopped broccoli
1 c. chicken broth
1 c. instant rice, uncooked
1/4 c. onion, chopped
10-3/4 oz. can cream of mushroom soup
8-oz. jar pasteurized process cheese sauce
6 T. margarine

Add frozen broccoli to a large bowl. Pour chicken broth over broccoli and stir until partially thawed. Stir in uncooked rice and onion; set aside. In a saucepan over low heat, combine mushroom soup, cheese sauce and margarine. Cook and stir until well blended. Spoon soup mixture over broccoli mixture; mix well. Transfer to a lightly greased 13"x9" baking pan. Bake, uncovered, at 300 degrees for one hour, or until hot and bubbly. Makes 4 to 6 servings.

For a no-fuss side dish that practically cooks itself, fill aluminum foil packets with sliced fresh veggies. Top with seasoning salt and 2 ice cubes; seal. Bake at 450 degrees for 20 to 25 minutes, or alongside a casserole at 350 degrees for a little longer. Delicious!

Working Woman's Mashed Potatoes

Judy Taylor
Butler, MO

My husband's aunt in Maryland fixed these potatoes when we were visiting her. She shared the recipe and I have made them many times. They are so handy to have in the refrigerator, or prepare them ahead for a family dinner.

5 lbs. redskin potatoes, peeled and quartered
8-oz. pkg. cream cheese, softened
1 c. sour cream
1/2 c. butter
salt and pepper to taste
Optional: 1 T. dried chives

Cover potatoes with water in a large saucepan. Bring to a boil over high heat; reduce heat to medium and cook until fork-tender. Drain; transfer potatoes to a large bowl. Add cream cheese, sour cream and butter while potatoes are still hot. Let stand to soften; mash to desired consistency. Add salt, pepper and chives, if desired. Serve immediately, or cover and refrigerate up to several days. May also be frozen. Makes 8 to 10 servings.

No matter what looms ahead, if you can eat today, enjoy today, mix good cheer with friends today, enjoy it and bless God for it.
– Henry Ward Beecher

Fresh & Tasty SIDES

Aunt Bev's Baked Beans

Jill Keaton
Fort Worth, TX

When I was a kid, we had this dish at all family gatherings, and of course we still have it now. I usually have to at least double the recipe because the original amounts aren't nearly enough! I like to add more bacon to the middle layer, because who would complain about more bacon?

2 16-oz. cans pork & beans
3/4 c. brown sugar, packed
1 to 2 t. dry mustard, to taste
6 slices bacon, diced and divided
1/2 c. catsup

Add one can beans to a greased 2-quart casserole dish; set aside. In a small bowl, combine brown sugar and mustard; sprinkle half of mixture over beans. Scatter half of bacon pieces on top. Add remaining can of beans; top with remaining brown sugar mixture. Spread catsup over the top; sprinkle with remaining bacon pieces. Bake, uncovered, at 325 degrees for 2-1/2 hours, or until bubbly and sauce is thickened. Makes 8 servings.

Bring out Mom's old printed tablecloths and use them...they're too much fun to hide away! Red strawberries, cowboys & cowgirls, vacation spots and other whimsical designs are sure to delight your kids and bring back fond memories of family meals years ago.

Southern-Style Green & Yellow Beans

Jackie Smulski
Lyons, IL

Traditional down-home goodness.

4 thick-cut slices bacon, or 6 slices regular-cut bacon
3/4 c. yellow or white onion, diced
3 cloves garlic, minced
1 lb. fresh green beans, ends trimmed
1 lb. fresh yellow wax beans, ends trimmed
3 c. reduced-sodium chicken broth
1/4 t. salt
1/2 t. pepper

Cook bacon in a large skillet over medium heat for 4 to 6 minutes, until golden. Add onion; cook for 5 minutes, stirring often. Add garlic and cook another one to 2 minutes. Add all beans and chicken broth; turn heat to medium-high and bring to a boil. Reduce heat to medium-low; season with salt and pepper. Cover and simmer for about 90 minutes, until beans are tender, checking after 45 minutes to avoid overcooking. Serve with a slotted spoon. Makes 4 to 6 servings.

Take the children along to a pick-your-own farm or local farmers' market. Bring home their selections and show them how to hull strawberries, shell peas and snap green beans. Memories in the making!

Fresh & Tasty SIDES

Pan-Roasted Vegetables

Debbie Benzi
Binghamton, NY

This is a healthy recipe that's easy to prepare and a hit wherever I take it! Perfect after a trip to the farmers' market.

1/3 c. butter
1/2 t. dried thyme
1/4 t. salt
1/4 t. pepper
7 c. sliced vegetables, like squash, zucchini, broccoli, cauliflower, peppers, etc.
2 small onions, quartered

Add butter to a 13"x9" baking pan; set in 400-degree oven until melted. Carefully remove pan from oven; stir seasonings into melted butter. Add vegetables; toss to coat. Cover with aluminum foil. Bake at 400 degrees for 22 to 27 minutes, until vegetables are crisp-tender. Makes 6 to 8 servings.

Creamed Lima Beans

Ann Farris
Biscoe, AR

Even if you don't like limas, you will love these! This recipe comes from a lady at my church, Saint Peter's on the Prairie... I finally got her to share it with me.

10-oz. pkg. frozen lima beans
1 T. butter
2 T. onion, chopped
1 T. all-purpose flour
salt and pepper to taste
1/2 c. milk
1 to 2 T. brown sugar, packed
1/2 c. sour cream
garlic powder to taste

Cook frozen beans according to package directions; drain well and set aside. Meanwhile, combine butter and onion in a saucepan; cook over medium heat until onion is tender. Sprinkle onion with flour, salt and pepper; stir until well blended. Slowly add milk and brown sugar; cook and stir until bubbly and well mixed. Stir in sour cream and cooked lima beans; heat through. Season with garlic powder and serve. Serves 4 to 6.

Cheesy Garlic-Roasted Asparagus

Lynne Doughan
Britt, IA

Here in Iowa in early spring, once the snow has melted, we jump in our old white pickup truck and hit the back-country roads, looking in the ditches, searching for wild asparagus. I recommend using more freshly ground black pepper than salt.

1 lb. fresh asparagus, ends snapped off
3 T. olive oil
1-1/2 T. garlic, minced
salt and pepper to taste
1 c. shredded mozzarella cheese
1/4 c. shredded Parmesan cheese

Spread asparagus evenly in a single layer on an ungreased large baking sheet; set aside. In a small bowl, whisk together oil and garlic; spoon evenly over asparagus. Using your hands, toss asparagus just until completely coated. Spread out into a single even layer; season lightly with salt and generously with pepper. Bake at 425 degrees for 15 minutes, or until asparagus is tender, but not yet wilted. Remove pan from oven; sprinkle evenly with cheeses and return to oven. Bake for another 2 minutes, or until cheese is completely melted. Turn on the broiler; broil just until cheese bubbles and begins to turn golden. Makes 4 servings.

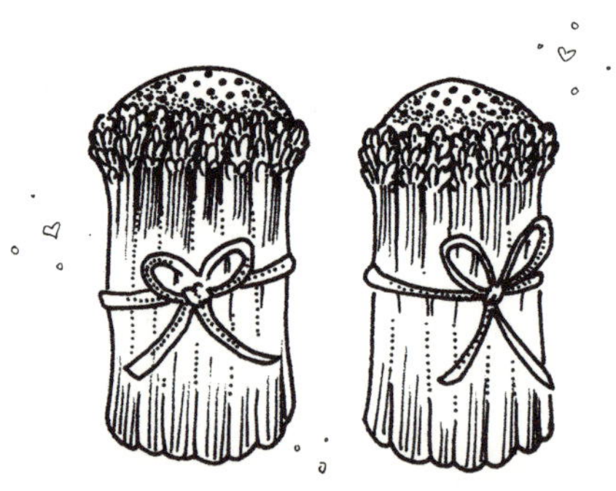

A flavorful drizzle for steamed veggies! In a saucepan, simmer 1/2 cup balsamic vinegar, stirring often, until thickened. So simple and scrumptious.

Fresh & Tasty SIDES

Baked Stuffed Tomatoes

Edward Kielar
Whitehouse, OH

During tomato season, we love to make baked tomatoes. Hope you give this a try!

4 large ripe tomatoes
salt to taste
1 egg, beaten
1 T. onion, minced
1 t. fresh parsley, minced
1/2 t. salt
1/8 t. pepper
1 c. soft bread crumbs, or seasoned croutons, crumbled
2 T. butter, melted

Cut a slice from the top of each tomato. Scoop out the pulp with a spoon, forming a shell. Sprinkle the insides of tomato shells with salt. Arrange tomatoes in a greased 9"x9" shallow baking pan; set aside. In a small bowl, lightly mix egg, onion, parsley, salt and pepper; spoon mixture into tomatoes. Add bread crumbs to another small bowl. Drizzle with melted butter; toss lightly to coat and sprinkle over tomatoes. Bake, uncovered, at 350 degrees about 30 minutes, until heated through. Serve hot. Makes 4 servings.

Dried herbs and spices add so much flavor to all kinds of dishes. Save money by buying them in the bulk food aisle, and buy big jars of the ones you use most often.

Babchi's Secret Potatoes

Paula Marchesi
Auburn, PA

"Babchi" means Grandma in Polish. Even though I never met my Babchi, she certainly passed down some delicious recipes which my mom passed on to me. This one is one of my favorites. She mixed together cabbage and potatoes in such a homey way that you really didn't know you were eating cabbage!

2-1/2 c. potatoes, peeled and cut into 1-inch cubes
2 c. cabbage, chopped
1 c. onion, chopped
1 t. salt
1/4 t. pepper
1/4 c. butter, softened
1 c. milk

Cover potatoes with water in a large stockpot. Bring to a boil over high heat; reduce heat to medium. Cover and cook for 8 to 10 minutes, until potatoes are almost tender. Do not drain. Add cabbage and onion to pot. Cover and simmer for 5 to 7 minutes, until cabbage is tender. Drain mixture and return to pot; add salt and pepper. Mash to desired consistency, gradually adding butter and milk. Makes 8 to 10 servings.

Potatoes can be peeled and cubed ahead of time. Simply cover them with water and add a splash of vinegar, and pop them in the refrigerator. They'll stay fresh and white.

Fresh & Tasty
SIDES

Grams' Haluski

Denise Sinclair
Smithtown, NY

This is a family Czechoslovakian cabbage & noodles recipe that my Grandmother made for Sunday dinners. It is still a family favorite that we continue to pass down through the generations! A helpful hint... cooking the cabbage slowly is the key.

1/4 c. butter, divided
1 c. onion, diced
1 large head cabbage, cut across into 1-inch slices
salt to taste
12-oz. pkg. wide or broad egg noodles, uncooked

In a large saucepan over medium heat, melt half the butter. Add onion; cook until caramelized and golden, about 10 minutes. Add cabbage and salt; reduce heat to low. Cook very slowly until cabbage cooks down and starts to brown. Meanwhile, cook noodles according to package directions; drain. Melt remaining butter in a skillet over medium heat; cook until browned. Add noodles and cooked cabbage to skillet; toss to mix well with butter and serve. Makes 8 servings.

If your kids refuse to eat cooked vegetables, try serving up colorful uncooked veggies with small cups of creamy yogurt, peanut butter or hummus for dunking. Problem solved!

Pepper Jack Corn Casserole

Dale Duncan
Waterloo, IA

My family loves the old-fashioned corn casserole I make for the holidays, so when I ran across this variation, I thought I'd give it a try. They loved it too! Now it's a go-to for our summer cookouts. Next time, I think I'll jazz it up even more with a can of Mexican sweet corn & diced peppers.

1 egg
15-1/4 oz. can corn, drained
14-3/4 oz. can cream-style corn
1-1/2 c. shredded Pepper Jack cheese, divided
1-1/4 c. round buttery crackers, crushed and divided
1/2 t. hot pepper sauce
1/4 t. salt
2 T. butter, melted

Beat egg in a large bowl; stir in all corn. Add one cup shredded cheese, 3/4 cup crushed crackers, hot sauce and salt; mix well. Spread evenly in a buttered 2-quart casserole dish; set aside. In a separate bowl, toss together remaining crackers, remaining cheese and melted butter; sprinkle evenly over casserole. Bake, uncovered, at 375 degrees for 45 minutes, or until bubbly and golden. Let stand 10 minutes before serving. Makes 6 servings.

Clean baked-on food from a casserole dish...no scrubbing needed! Place a dryer sheet in the dish and fill with warm water. Let the dish sit overnight, then sponge clean. The fabric softeners in the sheet will really soften the baked-on food!

Fresh & Tasty SIDES

Easy Spanish Rice

Teresa Eller
Denham Springs, LA

This recipe is great as a side dish, or rolled up in a flour tortilla.

2 T. canola oil
2 c. instant brown rice, uncooked
2 c. water
8-oz. can tomato sauce
1 onion, diced
1 green pepper, diced
1 t. chili powder
1 t. garlic powder
1 t. salt

Combine oil and uncooked rice in a 10" skillet with a tight-fitting lid. Sauté over medium heat for several minutes, just until rice is lightly golden. Stir in remaining ingredients. Cover and cook over low heat for 20 minutes without removing lid. Turn off heat; let stand for 5 minutes. Stir and serve. Makes 6 to 8 servings.

Mexican Sour Cream Rice

Geneva Rogers
Gillette, WY

We love this alongside enchiladas, and it's very easy to make. Mix in 1/4 cup chopped fresh cilantro, if you like.

14-oz. can chicken broth
1 c. long-cooking rice, uncooked
4-oz. can diced green chiles, drained
8-3/4 oz. can corn, drained
1 c. sour cream
1 c. shredded Monterey Jack cheese, divided
salt and pepper to taste

Bring chicken broth to a boil in a large saucepan over high heat; stir in rice. Reduce heat to low; cover and simmer for 20 minutes. Stir in chiles, corn, sour cream and 1/2 cup shredded cheese. Season with salt and pepper. Transfer to a lightly greased 1-1/2 quart casserole dish; top with remaining cheese. Bake, uncovered, at 350 degrees for 30 minutes, or until cheese is bubbly and lightly golden. Makes 6 servings.

Green Beans with Cherry Tomatoes

Vickie
Gooseberry Patch

A fresh, colorful veggie dish that reminds me of Grandma's garden.

1-1/2 lbs. fresh green beans, trimmed and cut into 2-inch pieces
1-1/2 c. water
1/4 c. butter
1 T. sugar
1-1/2 t. fresh basil, chopped
3/4 t. garlic salt
1/4 t. pepper
2 c. cherry tomatoes, cut in half

Combine beans and water in a large saucepan over medium heat. Bring to a boil; reduce heat to low. Simmer for about 10 minutes, until beans are tender. Drain and set aside. Meanwhile, melt butter in a skillet over medium heat. Stir in sugar, basil, garlic salt and pepper; add tomatoes. Cook, stirring occasionally, just until tomatoes are soft. Spoon tomato mixture over green beans; toss gently and serve. Makes 6 servings.

Start a tradition of hosting a regular night for dinner guests. Share your favorite comfort foods...it doesn't need to be fancy! Invite a neighbor or co-worker you've wanted to get to know better... encourage your kids to invite a friend. You'll be so glad you did!

Fresh & Tasty SIDES

Mom's Orange-Spiced Carrots

Sandy Coffey
Cincinnati, OH

Even the kids will eat these yummy carrots!

8 carrots, peeled and sliced
3 T. butter
1 c. orange juice
1/4 c. brown sugar, packed
1/8 t. cinnamon
1/2 t. nutmeg
2 oranges, peeled and sliced

Cover carrots with water in a saucepan over medium heat. Cook for 8 to 10 minutes, until carrots are fork-tender; drain and return to pan. Meanwhile, melt butter in a small saucepan over low heat; stir in orange juice and brown sugar until sugar dissolves. Spoon over carrots in pan; sprinkle with spices. Add orange slices. Simmer for a few minutes, until orange juice has almost evaporated. Makes 6 servings.

Grated citrus zest adds so much flavor to all kinds of recipes. Whenever you use an orange or lemon, grate the peel first. Keep it frozen in an airtight container for up to 2 months.

My Mom's Squash

Sandra Sebesta
Lockhart, TX

When I was a child growing up, my mom made this dish often, and it was one of my favorite things. You can use a combo of yellow squash and zucchini. It's so easy and so darn good!

4 yellow squash, sliced
2 T. water
2 to 3 T. butter
3 to 4 slices American cheese, cut into strips
salt and pepper to taste

Combine squash and water in a microwave-safe dish; cover with plastic. Microwave on high for 3 to 4 minutes, until soft; drain. Uncover; top with butter and cheese. Re-cover and let stand until melted. Season with salt and pepper. Serves 2 to 4.

Stovetop Baked Beans

Diane Hixon
Niceville, FL

Autumn is time for comfort foods, especially ones that include apple cider. This may be your favorite side from now on... and there's no baking involved!

8 slices bacon, chopped
1/4 c. onion, minced
2 16-oz. cans baked beans
1 c. apple cider
1/4 to 1/2 c. dark or golden raisins
1/2 t. cinnamon

Partially cook bacon in a skillet over medium heat. Remove bacon to paper towels; reserve 2 tablespoons drippings in skillet. Sauté onion in reserved drippings until tender; stir in undrained beans, cider, raisins and cinnamon. Mix in bacon; bring to a boil. Reduce heat to low and simmer for 20 to 25 minutes, stirring occasionally. Serves 6 to 8.

Too much zucchini? Grate extra zucchini and freeze it in 2-cup portions... it'll be ready to add to your favorite recipes all winter long.

Fresh & Tasty SIDES

Anne's Twice-Baked Potatoes

Caroline Miller
Nashville, TN

After a long day at school, it was always a special treat when my mom made these potatoes for dinner. They're simple to fix, but feel just a bit more decadent than an ordinary baked potato. These pair well with soup or salad, or any kind of grilled or roasted meat.

5 russet potatoes
1/2 c. butter
1/2 c. sour cream
1/2 c. shredded Cheddar or Mexican-blend cheese
2 t. salt

Pierce potatoes with a fork. Bake at 425 degrees for 45 minutes, or until fork-tender. Remove from oven; cool slightly. Cut each potato in half lengthwise. Scoop out cooked potato and place in a separate bowl, creating potato-skin shells. Add remaining ingredients to the cooked potato and mash well. Fill potato shells with potato mixture. Set filled shells on an ungreased baking sheet. Bake at 425 degrees for 15 to 20 minutes, until heated through and beginning to turn golden on top. Makes 5 to 10 servings.

Potatoes come in 3 basic types. Starchy russets bake up fluffy...great for frying, too. Round waxy potatoes are excellent in soups, casseroles and potato salads. All-purpose potatoes are in between and work well in most recipes. Do some delicious experimenting to find your favorites!

Stuffing Surprise

Edward Kielar
Whitehouse, OH

A great side dish anytime. The secret ingredient is yellow squash!

8-1/2 oz. pkg. corn muffin mix
2 c. yellow squash, sliced
3/4 c. onion, chopped
1/4 c. butter
3 eggs, beaten
10-3/4 oz. can cream of chicken soup
1/4 t. salt
1/8 t. pepper

Bake corn muffin mix according to package directions, using an 8"x8" baking pan. Set aside to cool. Meanwhile, in a large skillet over medium heat, sauté squash and onion in butter until tender. Remove from heat; stir in 4 cups crumbled cornbread and remaining ingredients. Transfer to a greased one-quart casserole dish. Bake, uncovered, at 350 degrees for 40 minutes, or until heated through. Makes 6 servings.

Make your own bread crumbs for crunchy casserole toppings and stuffing. Save extra bread slices (leftover "heels" are fine) and freeze. When you have enough, bake the slices in a 250-degree oven until dry and crumbly, then tear into sections and pulse in a food processor or blender. Simple and thrifty!

Easy Cornbread Stuffing

Barbara Klein
Newburgh, IN

I love this stuffing. It is delicious and very easy to make.

2 6-oz. pkgs. cornbread stuffing mix
3 slices white bread, toasted and torn into pieces
3 stalks celery, chopped
1 c. onion, chopped
1 egg, beaten
dried sage to taste
Optional: 14-oz. can chicken broth

In a large saucepan, prepare stuffing mixes according to package directions. Add remaining ingredients and mix well, adding chicken broth as desired if a moister consistency is desired. Transfer to a greased 13"x9" baking pan. Bake, uncovered, at 350 degrees for 30 to 45 minutes, until lightly golden. Makes 10 servings.

Bouillon cubes are handy whenever broth is called for in a recipe. For one cup of broth, dissolve a bouillon cube in one cup of boiling water. A 14-ounce can of broth equals 1-3/4 cups prepared bouillon.

Steakhouse Rice

Sarah Slaven
Strunk, KY

This is my husband's favorite rice. I fix it often...it is a good side dish for just about anything!

1/2 c. butter
4 c. instant rice, uncooked
1/2 c. onion, diced
2 T. dried parsley
2 to 3 t. smoked paprika
2 to 3 t. garlic powder
1/4 t. red pepper flakes
4 c. chicken broth

Melt butter in a saucepan over medium heat. Stir in uncooked rice, onion and seasonings. Sauté until rice is golden, stirring often. Mix in chicken broth; bring to a boil. Remove from heat; cover and let stand for 5 to 10 minutes. Fluff rice with a fork and serve. Makes 6 servings.

Scrumptious Spinach Casserole

Christine Wheeler
Jupiter, FL

This has become one of my favorite recipes, ever since I found it several years ago. It is delicious and very easy to make.

2 c. frozen chopped spinach, thawed
1 c. shredded mozzarella cheese
2 T. butter, softened
1 egg, beaten
10-3/4 oz. can cream of mushroom soup
1 c. seasoned salad croutons, any flavor

Squeeze out as much liquid from spinach as possible; add spinach to a microwave-safe bowl. Microwave on high for one to 2 minutes, until warmed. Add cheese and butter; mix very well. Stir in egg and mushroom soup; mix in croutons. Spread mixture evenly in a buttered 13"x9" baking pan. Bake, uncovered, at 350 degrees for 40 to 45 minutes, until golden. Serves 8 to 12.

Store tomatoes stem-side down on the kitchen counter for fresh-from-the-garden taste.

Fresh & Tasty SIDES

Yummy Squash Casserole

Pam Massey
Marshall, AR

This tasty side goes together in a jiffy! Use your favorite boxed corn muffin mix. I sometimes use a cast-iron skillet for baking to give a nice crisp texture.

2 to 3 yellow squash, finely chopped or shredded
1 onion, finely chopped or shredded
salt and pepper to taste
1 egg, beaten
8-1/2 oz. pkg. corn muffin mix
1/2 c. milk, or more as needed
Optional: 1 c. shredded Cheddar cheese

Combine squash and onion in a bowl; season with salt and pepper. Add egg; beat until well blended. Add dry corn muffin mix; stir until well combined. Add milk; stir well. If desired, fold in cheese. Pour into a well-oiled 13"x9" baking pan. Bake, uncovered, at 375 degrees for 35 to 45 minutes, until set and golden. Serves 8.

Frozen vegetables come in so many different varieties. Fill the freezer with your family's favorites and you'll always be ready to whip up a delicious side dish in a jiffy.

Creamy Cauliflower Bake

Marian Forck
Jefferson City, MO

This is really good made with fresh cauliflower from the garden. The recipe was taken from the Missouri Secretary of State's cookbook from 1992. We all loved sharing our special recipes at work.

1-1/2 c. cauliflower, cut into bite-size flowerets
10-3/4 oz. can cream of mushroom soup
1/4 c. milk
1/2 c. shredded Cheddar cheese
1 c. biscuit baking mix
1/4 c. butter, melted

Cover cauliflower with water in a saucepan over medium heat. Cook until crisp-tender; drain. Transfer cauliflower to an ungreased 2-quart casserole dish; set aside. In a bowl, whisk together mushroom soup and milk until smooth; spoon over cauliflower. Sprinkle with cheese. In a small bowl, stir together baking mix and butter until crumbly; sprinkle over cheese. Bake, uncovered, at 400 degrees for 20 minutes, or until hot and bubbly. Serves 6 to 8.

Sesame Green Beans

Irene Robinson
Cincinnati, OH

This is an ideal accompaniment to almost any main dish. It couldn't be easier to fix!

1 lb. fresh green beans, trimmed
2 cloves garlic, minced
1 T. sesame seed
2 T. canola oil
salt to taste

In a saucepan, cover green beans with water; bring to a boil. Cook, uncovered, for 8 to 10 minutes, until crisp-tender. Meanwhile, in a skillet over medium heat, sauté garlic and sesame seed in oil. Drain beans; stir in garlic mixture. Season with salt and serve. Serves 6.

Pick up a vintage divided serving dish... just right for serving up a choice of sides.

Can't-Miss COMFORT FOOD MEALS

Jacki's Chicken Enchiladas

Jacki Smith
Fayetteville, NC

An easy, cheesy recipe to make with rotisserie chicken. Tasty with Mexican rice and sweet corn...my family always asks for more!

6 6-inch flour tortillas
2 to 3 c. deli rotisserie chicken, shredded
1 onion, chopped
8-oz. pkg. shredded Cheddar cheese, divided
10-3/4 oz. can cream of chicken soup
10-3/4 oz. can cream of celery soup
4-oz. can diced green chiles
2 c. sour cream, divided

Stack tortillas on a microwave-safe plate; cover with a dampened paper towel. Microwave for one minute, or until warmed. Spoon chicken evenly into the center of each tortilla. Divide onion and one cup cheese evenly among tortillas. Roll up filled tortillas. Arrange in a greased 13"x9" baking pan; set aside. In a large bowl, stir together soups, chiles and one cup sour cream; spoon over tortillas in pan. Top with remaining cheese. Bake, uncovered, at 350 degrees for 45 minutes, or until bubbly and cheese is melted. Serve with remaining sour cream. Makes 6 servings.

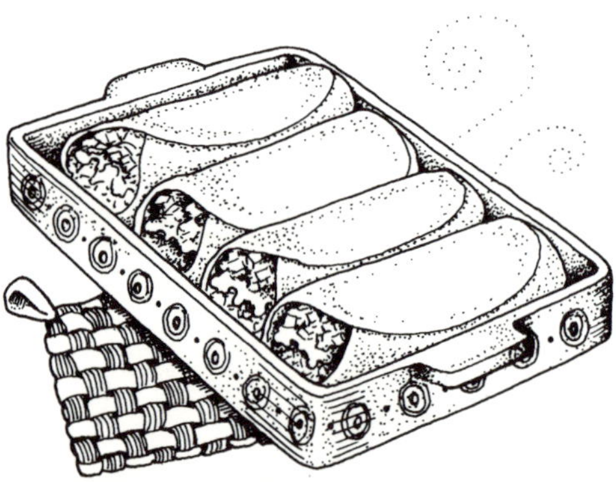

Shake up a tasty dressing for lettuce, tomato and avocado chopped salads. In a covered jar, combine 3 tablespoons olive oil, 2 tablespoons lime juice, 1/4 teaspoon dry mustard and 1/2 teaspoon salt. Cover and shake until well blended.

Sharon's Beef Casserole Supreme

Marian Forck
Jefferson City, MO

I got this recipe from my friend Sharon. It's so good, you may want to make a double batch! Add a fresh vegetable and some spiced applesauce, and you have a terrific meal.

1 lb. ground beef
3/4 c. onion, chopped
1 clove garlic, chopped
1/2 t. salt
1/2 t. pepper
2 T. catsup
10-3/4 oz. can cream of chicken soup
8-oz. pkg. cream cheese, softened
7-1/2 oz. tube refrigerated biscuits

In a skillet over medium-low heat, combine beef, onion, garlic, salt and pepper. Cook for about 20 minutes, until onion is clear and beef is browned; drain. Add catsup, chicken soup and cream cheese, stirring after each addition. Spoon into a 1-1/2 quart casserole dish sprayed with non-stick vegetable spray. Top with biscuits. Bake, uncovered, at 350 degrees for 20 minutes, or until bubbly and biscuits are golden. Makes 6 servings.

Speed up prep time on ground beef recipes! Brown several pounds of beef, adding seasonings and chopped onions if you like. Divide into one-pound portions in large plastic freezer bags and flatten to freeze. To use, thaw overnight in the fridge.

Italian Sausage Fettuccine

Sonja Meyer
Harper, TX

This is a go-to recipe for our family that my mom got from her friend Gwynne...we all loved it! Serve with a crisp green salad and bread sticks.

1 lb. ground pork Italian sausage
13-3/4 oz. can quartered artichoke hearts in water, drained
8-oz. can sliced mushrooms, drained
3.8-oz. can sliced black olives, drained
6.7-oz. jar pesto sauce
16-oz. pkg. fettuccine pasta, uncooked
Garnish: grated Parmesan cheese

Brown sausage in a large skillet over medium heat; drain. Add artichokes, mushrooms, olives and pesto sauce; stir well. Reduce heat to low. Cook, stirring occasionally, until well blended and heated through. Meanwhile, cook pasta according to package directions; drain. Toss cooked pasta with sausage mixture; top with Parmesan cheese and serve. Makes 4 to 6 servings.

For flavorful, fast-fix garlic bread, brush Italian bread slices with softened butter. Sprinkle with garlic & herb seasoning blend and broil until golden. Try it with leftover hamburger buns, too!

Vegetarian Pasta Alfredo

Peter Stadelman
Williamsville, NY

Good if you're short on time and money...we think it's just as delicious as shrimp or chicken Alfredo!

16-oz. pkg. whole-wheat penne pasta, uncooked
2 15-oz. jars Alfredo sauce
14-1/2 oz. can diced tomatoes with Italian seasoning
8-oz. can sliced mushrooms, drained

Cook pasta according to package directions; drain and transfer to a large bowl. Add Alfredo sauce, tomatoes with juice and mushrooms. Toss gently; serve warm. Makes 4 to 6 servings.

Baked Penne Pasta

Jennie Gist
Gooseberry Patch

An old favorite! Try it with curly rotini pasta, too.

16-oz. pkg. penne pasta, uncooked
2 24-oz. jars spaghetti sauce
1-1/2 c. shredded mozzarella cheese, divided
Garnish: grated Parmesan cheese
Optional: 2 T. fresh basil, chopped

Cook pasta according to package instructions; drain. Transfer pasta to a greased 2-quart casserole dish. Add pasta sauce and 3/4 cup mozzarella cheese; mix gently. Cover with aluminum foil; bake at 375 degrees for 20 minutes. Uncover; sprinkle with remaining cheese and bake for another 5 minutes, or until cheese is melted. Top with Parmesan cheese and basil, as desired. Makes 6 servings.

Just for fun, try a different pasta shape with your favorite pasta recipe!

Carolyn's String Pie

Carolyn Deckard
Bedford, IN

This dish was one of my kids' favorite ways to eat spaghetti. Serve with a tossed salad and bread sticks for a tasty meal.

8-oz. pkg. spaghetti, uncooked
1 lb. ground beef
1/2 c. onion, chopped
1/4 c. green pepper, chopped
24-oz. jar spaghetti sauce
1/3 c. grated Parmesan cheese
2 eggs, beaten
2 t. butter, melted
1 c. cottage cheese
1/2 c. shredded mozzarella cheese

Cook spaghetti according to package directions; drain. Meanwhile, cook beef, onion and green pepper in a large skillet over medium-high heat until beef is browned; drain. Stir in spaghetti sauce; remove from heat. In a large bowl, combine cooked spaghetti, Parmesan cheese, eggs and butter. Mix well; spread evenly in a lightly greased 13"x9" baking pan. Spread cottage cheese over top. Cover with sauce mixture; sprinkle with mozzarella cheese. Bake, uncovered, at 350 degrees for about 20 minutes, until bubbly and heated through. Makes 6 to 8 servings.

Make a scrapbook of Mom's favorite recipes...just going through the recipe box together will stir up sweet memories. Choose your favorites, make copies and add family photos. Taken to the nearest copy shop, duplicates can quickly and easily be made to share with family & friends.

French Onion Chicken Casserole

Emilie Britton
New Bremen, OH

This creamy chicken casserole gets a flavor boost from crunchy slivered almonds and French fried onions. Serve with a side salad and you have a delicious meal!

10-3/4 oz. can cream of chicken soup
1 c. sour cream
1 c. mayonnaise
1 c. shredded Cheddar cheese
3 c. cooked chicken, chopped
1 c. celery, chopped
1/2 c. slivered almonds
6-oz. can French fried onions

In a large bowl, stir together chicken soup, sour cream, mayonnaise and cheese. Add chicken, celery and almonds; stir to combine well and spread evenly in a greased 13"x9" baking pan. Bake, uncovered, at 350 degrees for 30 minutes, or until bubbly. Remove from oven; sprinkle with onions and bake for another 5 minutes. Let stand for 5 to 10 minutes before serving. Makes 6 to 8 servings.

For juicy, flavorful chicken, cover with water and simmer gently until cooked through, then turn off the heat and let the chicken cool in its own broth.

Ann's Baked Pork Chops

Linda Finfrock
Cary, NC

A favorite easy pork recipe, shared by my Aunt Ann years ago. She was a great cook. The recipe can easily be cut in half for two people. I've also made this with sliced pork tenderloin.

6 bone-in or boneless pork chops
1 t. salt
1/2 t. pepper
small amount oil for frying
15-oz. can tomato sauce
1/2 c. water
1/2 c. celery, chopped
2 T. brown sugar, packed
1 T. lemon juice
1 t. dry mustard

Season pork chops with salt and pepper. In a skillet over medium heat, brown pork chops in oil on both sides; drain. Arrange pork chops in a shallow 13"x9" baking pan coated with non-stick vegetable spray. Combine remaining ingredients in a bowl; spoon over pork chops. Cover and bake at 350 degrees for one hour, or until pork chops are done. Makes 4 to 6 servings.

When pan-frying meat, you'll get the best results if the pan isn't overcrowded. Use an extra-large skillet, or cook in 2 batches.

Skillet Sausage Supper

Beckie Apple
Grannis, AR

Throughout the nearly 50 years I've worked while managing my home and taking care of my husband and son, I learned many shortcuts for evening meals. This skillet meal is a favorite...delicious with a chopped salad and fresh bread.

2 T. oil
4 russet potatoes, peeled and thinly sliced
1 onion, thinly sliced
1 green pepper, thinly sliced
1/2 t. salt
1/4 t. pepper
14-oz. pkg. Kielbasa sausage, sliced 1-inch thick

In a deep skillet over medium heat, combine all ingredients except sausage. Cook until vegetables are fork-tender. Add sausage; toss well and reduce to medium-low heat. Cover and simmer for 10 minutes, or until sausage is browned. Makes 4 to 6 servings.

Season an old cast-iron skillet to make it practically non-stick. Brush a thin coat of canola oil all over the skillet and bake it at 300 degrees for one hour. Then turn off the heat and let the skillet cool completely in the oven...that's all it takes!

Raised Meatballs

Kathryn Boglovits
Kernersville, NC

A simple, easy recipe that my husband loves. You can add some mushrooms or onions before baking if you wish, but we like it just the way it is. Serve meatballs over steamed rice or mashed potatoes, topped with the gravy from the pan.

4 slices day-old bread, crusts trimmed if desired
1 egg, beaten
1/2 c. milk
1/2 t. baking powder
1 t. salt
1/2 t. pepper
1 lb. ground beef
oil for frying
10-3/4 oz. can cream of mushroom soup
10-3/4 oz. can cream of chicken soup
1-1/4 c. milk

Cut bread slices into cubes; set aside. In a large bowl, mix together egg, milk, baking power, salt and pepper. Add bread cubes; toss to mix well. Let stand until all milk is absorbed and bread is mushy. Add beef and mix well, using your hands. Form into 1-1/2 inch meatballs. Heat a small amount of oil in a skillet over medium heat. Add meatballs, a few at a time; cook until browned on all sides. Transfer meatballs to a lightly greased 9"x9" baking pan; set aside. In a large bowl, whisk together soups and milk; spoon over meatballs. Bake, uncovered, at 350 degrees for one hour. Serves 6.

Russet and Yukon Gold potatoes are perfect for making delicious mashed potatoes. Whip in a teaspoon or so of baking powder... they'll be extra light and fluffy.

Chicken Marsala

Shirley Howie
Foxboro, MA

This is a great dish for entertaining, as the wine gives it such a rich flavor. It also makes an easy weeknight meal, using chicken broth instead of the wine. Either way, this recipe is scrumptious!

5 boneless, skinless chicken breast cutlets
1/2 c. all-purpose flour
1/4 t. garlic powder
1/2 t. salt
1/4 t. pepper
1 T. butter
2 T. olive oil
8-oz. pkg. sliced mushrooms
2 cloves garlic, minced
3/4 c. Marsala wine or chicken broth
cooked pasta or steamed rice

Pound chicken to flatten slightly; set aside. In a shallow dish, mix flour and seasonings. Coat chicken pieces with flour mixture. Melt butter with olive oil in a skillet over medium-high heat. Add mushrooms and garlic; cook for 5 minutes, stirring often. Add chicken to skillet. Cook about 8 minutes, turning once, until lightly golden. Stir in wine or chicken broth. Cover and cook for 8 to 10 minutes, until juices run clear when chicken is pierced. Serve chicken over cooked pasta or rice. Makes 5 servings.

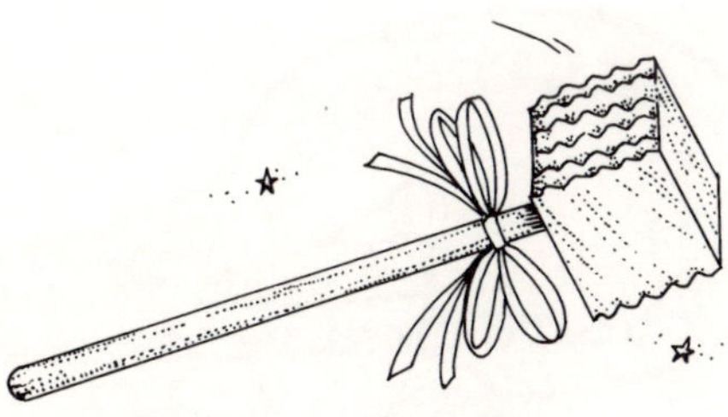

Boneless chicken breasts are a terrific choice for speedy meals. They'll cook up even quicker if placed in a large plastic zipping bag and flattened with a meat mallet.

Chicken & Noodle Casserole

Tina Matie
Alma, GA

This is a great comfort food that takes no time to fix. To me, this casserole has all the elements of my favorite homestyle soup, sprinkled with cheese and baked until bubbly and golden.

2 c. medium egg noodles, uncooked
10-3/4 oz. can cream of chicken soup
1/2 c. milk
1 c. frozen peas
12-1/2 oz. can white chunk chicken breast, drained
1/2 c. shredded sharp Cheddar cheese
salt and pepper to taste
2 T. dry bread crumbs
1 T. butter, melted

Cook noodles according to package directions; drain. Meanwhile, in a lightly greased 1-1/2 quart casserole dish, stir together chicken soup, milk, frozen peas, chicken and cheese. Fold in cooked noodles; season with salt and pepper. Bake, uncovered, at 400 degrees for 20 minutes, or until bubbly and heated through. Remove from oven; stir chicken mixture in pan. Mix together bread crumbs and melted butter in a cup; sprinkle over mixture in pan. Bake for another 10 minutes, or until golden. Makes 4 servings.

Good china isn't just for the holidays or special celebrations... use it to make everyday family meals a little more special!

Chicken Murdock

Donna Parks
Jacksonville, TX

My mother was a beautician, so she needed quick & easy dishes. This one was my favorite...I have reworked it to suit my family.

2 12-1/2 oz. cans white chicken breast, drained
26-oz. can cream of chicken soup
16-oz. pkg. pasteurized process cheese, cubed
2-oz. jar diced pimentos, drained
1/4 c. butter, melted
salt and pepper to taste
16-oz. pkg. wide egg noodles, cooked

In a large bowl, combine all ingredients except noodles; mix well. Transfer to a lightly greased 3-quart casserole dish. Bake, uncovered, at 350 degrees for 30 to 45 minutes, until bubbly and heated through. Serve over cooked noodles. Makes 6 to 8 servings.

Turn leftovers into plan-overs! Plan 2 meals that use some of the same ingredients. Extra baked chicken can become shredded chicken sandwiches another night...extra taco beef can be stirred into a pot of chili. The possibilities are endless and real time-savers.

Tuna Casserole

Barbara Wener
West Hartford, CT

Everyone likes this quick dish...it's good for lunch or supper!

2 stalks celery, chopped
1 onion, chopped
1 green pepper, chopped
2 to 3 t. butter
5-oz. can chow mein noodles, divided
12-oz. can white tuna, drained
10-3/4 oz. can cream of mushroom soup
2 4-oz. cans sliced mushrooms, drained
1 c. cashews

In a skillet over medium heat, sauté vegetables in butter. Spread mixture in a buttered 2-quart casserole dish. Spread half of noodles evenly over vegetables; set aside. Combine remaining ingredients in a bowl; mix well and spread evenly over noodles. Top with remaining noodles. Bake, uncovered, at 350 degrees for one hour, or until hot and bubbly. Makes 4 to 6 servings.

Keep the pantry stocked with canned vegetables, creamy soups, rice mixes, pasta and other handy meal-makers. If you pick up 2 or 3 items whenever they're on sale, you'll have a full pantry in no time at all!

Pecan-Crusted Salmon

Elizabeth McCollough
Winter Haven, FL

Once, my husband took me to this great little restaurant called Mara Lisa Cove, out in the backwoods of Lake Wales, Florida. It has since closed, but this was our first date and the food was just amazing. We love making this simple recipe together because it brings back sweet memories of our first date, over 20 years ago. We have even cooked the salmon on a Blackstone grill. Steamed veggies and rice go well with this.

4 4-oz. salmon fillets, skin removed
3 eggs, beaten
1 c. pecan pieces, finely chopped

Dredge salmon fillets in beaten egg, coating well. Roll each fillet in pecan pieces, coating very well. Arrange salmon in a lightly greased 9"x9" baking pan. Bake, uncovered, at 325 degrees for 19 minutes, or until fish flakes easily with a fork. Serves 4.

Honey-Citrus Salmon

JoAnn
Gooseberry Patch

Delicious anytime with a big salad, and oh-so easy to fix!

4 6-oz. salmon fillets, skin on
salt and pepper to taste
1/4 c. honey
3 T. lime juice
2 T. orange juice

Arrange salmon fillets skin-side down in a greased 9"x9" baking pan. Season with salt and pepper; set aside. In a cup, stir together honey and juices until well blended; spoon over salmon. Bake, uncovered, at 400 degrees for 10 to 12 minutes, until fish flakes easily with a fork. Serves 4.

Stir diced, sautéed mushrooms, onions or celery into prepared wild rice mix for a homemade touch.

Super-Easy Pantry Beef Stroganoff

Sheila Peregrin
Lancaster, PA

My adult daughters always liked to have this crockpot meal when they were home from college...comfort food that they now make in their own homes! This is wonderful served with 3-bean salad or coleslaw. Sometimes I use sliced fresh mushrooms instead of canned, if I have them on hand. I'll also add some sliced onions or a little garlic at the beginning of the cooking process.

1 lb. stew beef cubes
10-3/4 oz. can cream of mushroom soup
3/4 c. water
4-oz. can sliced mushrooms, drained
salt and pepper to taste
12-oz. pkg. wide egg noodles, uncooked
8-oz. container sour cream

In a 4-quart crockpot, combine beef cubes, mushroom soup, water and mushrooms. Mix well; season with salt and pepper, as desired. Cover and cook on low setting for 6 to 8 hours, until beef is tender. Shortly before serving time, cook noodles as package directs; drain. Stir sour cream into beef mixture. Spoon beef mixture over noodles; stir to combine and serve. Makes 4 servings.

Cook egg noodles the easy way, no watching needed. Bring water to a rolling boil, then turn off heat. Add noodles and let stand for 20 minutes, stirring twice. Drain well and toss with a little butter...ready to serve!

Crockpot Creamy Ham & Broccoli

Sharon Theisen
St. Cloud, MN

A favorite change from hamburger, and it's simple to make!

10-3/4 oz. can cream of mushroom soup
8-oz. jar pasteurized process cheese spread
1 c. milk
16-oz. pkg. frozen cut broccoli, thawed and well drained
3 c. cooked ham, cubed
8-oz. can sliced water chestnuts, drained
1 c. instant rice, uncooked
1/2 c. celery, chopped
1/4 t. pepper

Spray a 5-quart crockpot with non-stick vegetable spray; whisk together mushroom soup, cheese spread and milk in crock. Add remaining ingredients; mix well. Cover and cook on low setting for 4 to 5 hours, until hot and bubbly. Makes 4 to 6 servings.

Set out all the fixin's for a baked potato bar for dinner tonight! Let the kids choose their favorite toppers...a fun way to serve a satisfying, simple meal.

Sweet-and-Sour Chicken

Teresa Eller
Denham Springs, LA

This is one of my favorites! I like to serve it with chicken-fried rice and homemade egg rolls. For good results, cut the chicken and veggies into chunks that are similar in size.

- 2 to 3 lbs. chicken tenders, cut into chunks
- 1 T. canola oil
- 1 onion, cut into chunks
- 6 to 8 carrots, peeled and cut into chunks
- 1 green pepper, cut into chunks
- 1 c. broccoli flowerets
- 1 c. cauliflower flowerets
- 20-oz. can pineapple chunks, drained
- 14-oz. jar sweet-and-sour sauce

In a large cast-iron skillet over medium heat, sauté chicken in oil until no longer pink. Add onion and carrots; cook to desired tenderness. Add green pepper, broccoli and cauliflower; cook to desired tenderness. Add pineapple and sweet-and-sour sauce; stir to coat well. Cover and simmer for about 10 minutes, until all the ingredients have finished cooking and pineapple is hot. Do not overcook. Makes 6 to 8 servings.

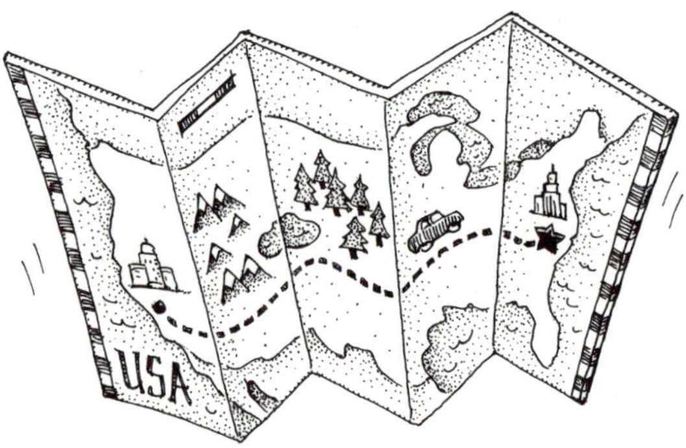

Host an adventure potluck...a terrific way to get together with friends old & new. Ask each guest to bring a favorite dish from their hometown, whether that's somewhere across the USA or even around the world. Remember to ask everyone to bring recipe cards to share!

Egg Roll Skillet

Kathleen Craig
Burlington, WI

We like homemade egg rolls, but my arthritis prevents me from making egg rolls, so this became my solution. Very tasty!

3 c. cooked chicken, shredded
1 t. ground ginger
1/2 t. garlic salt
8-oz. jar sliced mushrooms, drained
14-oz. pkg. coleslaw mix
1/4 c. soy sauce
Garnish: sliced green onions

Add shredded chicken to a lightly greased large skillet over medium heat. Sprinkle with seasonings; add mushrooms and coleslaw mix. Cook, stirring often, until mushrooms are golden. Stir in soy sauce; heat through. Serve topped with green onions. Makes 4 servings.

Spicy Chicken Mac & Cheese

Dawn Smith
Cape Girardeau, MO

One night, as a tired teacher with two little boys, I scanned my pantry and tossed this together. It was a hit...yum! Always goes quickly at potlucks, too.

12-oz. pkg. elbow macaroni, uncooked
16-oz. jar pasteurized process cheese sauce
2 12-oz. cans white chicken breast, drained
14-1/2 oz. can diced tomatoes with green chiles, drained

Cook macaroni according to package directions, just until tender. Drain; return macaroni to pan and mix in remaining ingredients. Cook over low heat, stirring occasionally, until well mixed and heated through. Serves 6.

Ah! There is nothing like staying at home for real comfort.
– Jane Austin

30-Minute Skillet Lasagna

Barbara Cebula
Chicopee, MA

I found this recipe and gave it a try...my husband likes it better than lasagna baked in the oven! If you are not a fan of cottage cheese, ricotta cheese may be used in its place.

1/2 lb. ground beef
1/2 c. yellow or white onion, diced
2 cloves garlic, chopped
1/2 t. salt
2 c. jarred marinara sauce
1-1/2 to 2 c. water, divided
8 lasagna noodles, uncooked and broken up
1 c. cottage cheese
1 c. shredded mozzarella cheese

Brown and crumble beef in a large skillet over medium heat. Stir in onion, garlic and salt; sauté for about 5 minutes, until onion is translucent. Drain; stir in marinara sauce and 1-1/2 cups water. Increase heat to medium-high and bring to a boil. Reduce heat to low; nestle the broken noodles into the sauce. Cover skillet and simmer for 10 minutes. Uncover; scrape up any browned bits that have stuck to the bottom. Stir in remaining water if mixture looks dry. Stir in cottage cheese; sprinkle with mozzarella cheese. Cover and simmer an additional 10 to 12 minutes, until noodles are tender. Let stand, uncovered, for 5 to 10 minutes before serving. Makes 5 servings.

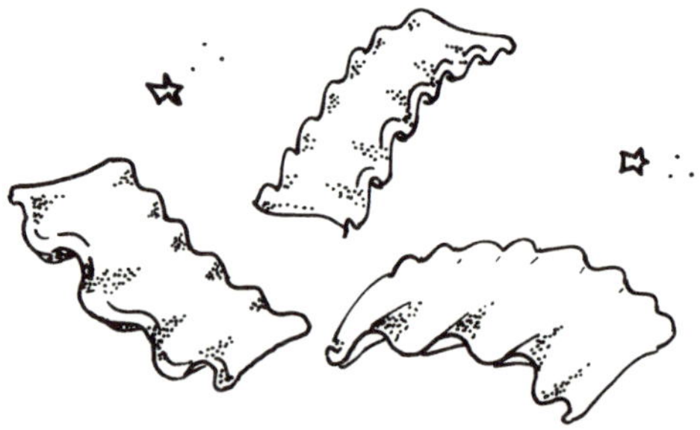

Keep a few packages of frozen ravioli tucked in the freezer for easy meal-making anytime. Quickly cooked and topped with your favorite jar sauce, it's terrific as either a side dish or a meatless main.

Spaghetti with Olive Oil & Garlic Sauce

Annette Ceravolo
Birmingham, AL

My mom made this often, with four children close in age growing up. Something quick, easy and delicious.

1/2 c. extra-virgin oil
4 cloves garlic, minced
1/2 c. water
1 T. fresh parsley, chopped
1/2 t. pepper
16-oz. pkg. spaghetti, uncooked

Heat oil in a large skillet over medium heat. Add garlic and cook until golden. Remove skillet from heat and cool slightly. Return to heat; slowly stir in water, parsley and pepper. Simmer and stir for about 10 minutes. Remove from heat; set aside. Meanwhile, cook spaghetti according to package directions; drain. Add spaghetti to skillet and heat through. Makes 4 to 6 servings.

Beefy Rotini Skillet

Jill Burton
Gooseberry Patch

Easy-peasy...you'll be serving dinner in no time at all!

8-oz. pkg. rotini pasta, uncooked
1 lb. ground sirloin beef
24-oz. can spaghetti sauce
6-oz. can tomato paste
1 c. shredded mozzarella cheese

Cook pasta according to package directions; drain. Meanwhile, brown beef in a large skillet over medium heat; drain. Add spaghetti sauce and tomato paste to beef; stir well. Reduce heat to medium-low; simmer beef mixture for 5 minutes, stirring occasionally. Stir cooked pasta into beef mixture; sprinkle with cheese. Cover and cook another 5 minutes, or until cheese melts. Serves 4.

Florence's Burrito Filling

Marion Sundberg
Oak Hills, CA

My mom always made this dish after we'd had roast beef or grilled steak, using the leftover meat. For years, this was the only burrito filling that I knew of. It's not Mexican-style, more of a midwestern version. I make this and all my kids do too. It's a family favorite and great way to use leftover beef. And you put it all in your crockpot, so it's super easy!

2 c. leftover roast beef or grilled steak, chopped
4 small potatoes, peeled and cubed
4-oz. can diced green chiles
1-1/4 c. beef broth or water
10-1/2 oz. can French onion soup
6 8-inch flour tortillas
Garnish: sour cream, shredded cheese

Combine beef, potatoes, chiles, water or broth and soup in a 4-quart crockpot. Cover and cook on low setting for 8 hours, or on high setting for 4 hours. Serve beef mixture on warmed tortillas, garnished as desired. Makes 6 servings.

Whip up a side dish pronto for your next Mexican meal! Prepare instant rice, using chicken broth instead of water. Stir in a generous dollop of salsa, top with shredded cheese and cover for a few minutes, until the cheese melts.

Chicken Diablo

Robert Forrest
Fairview, OR

This recipe is so simple and tasty, I wanted to share it with everyone! It's easy, fast and good.

4 to 6 chicken thighs and/or drumsticks
1/2 c. honey
1/4 c. yellow or Dijon mustard
1/4 c. butter, melted
1 t. curry powder
1 t. garlic powder
salt and pepper to taste

Arrange chicken pieces in a greased 13"x9" baking pan; set aside. Mix together remaining ingredients in a bowl; spoon over chicken. Bake, uncovered, at 375 degrees for about 40 minutes, or until golden and chicken juices run clear when pierced. Serves 4 to 6.

Try barley pilaf instead of rice or noodles on the side. Simply prepare quick-cooking barley with chicken broth instead of water. Season with a little chopped onion and dried parsley. Tasty and filling!

Grandma's Goulash

Katie Bonomo
Danville, IL

Every time I make this dish, I think of my grandma. This was my favorite recipe of hers that she made. Grandma always put a dollop of sour cream on hers. Just smelling it cooking brings back so many great memories, and I feel like I'm in Grandma's kitchen all over again.

2 lbs. ground beef
1 onion, chopped
2 T. Italian seasoning
1 T. Worcestershire sauce
4 cloves garlic, minced
1 t. pepper
29-oz. can tomato sauce
2 14-1/2 oz. cans diced tomatoes, drained
2 bay leaves
16-oz. pkg. elbow macaroni, uncooked
Garnish: sour cream

Brown beef with onion in a large stockpot over medium heat; drain. Sprinkle with Italian seasoning, Worcestershire sauce, garlic and pepper; simmer for about 5 minutes. Stir in tomato sauce, tomatoes and bay leaves; cook until bubbly. Reduce heat to medium-low. Simmer for at least one hour, stirring occasionally. About 20 minutes before serving, discard bay leaves. Cook macaroni according to package directions; drain and stir into mixture in stockpot. Serve garnished with sour cream. Makes 10 servings.

Remove bay leaves easily after cooking...tuck them into a metal tea ball that can hang on the side of the pot.

Ham & Noodle Casserole

Patricia Nau
River Grove, IL

Leftover baked ham from the holidays? No problem! This is a scrumptious way to make it disappear. Voilà!

12-oz. pkg. broad no-yolk noodles, uncooked
3 T. butter
4 eggs, separated
1-1/2 c. cooked ham, cubed
1 c. sour cream
2 green onions, chopped
2 T. fresh parsley, chopped
salt and pepper to taste

Cook noodles according to package directions; drain and toss with butter. Meanwhile, in a large bowl, beat egg yolks until thickened. Add egg yolks to cooked noodles along with ham, sour cream, onions, parsley and seasonings; mix well and set aside. In another bowl, with an electric mixer on medium speed, beat egg whites until stiff peaks form; gently fold into noodle mixture. Spoon mixture into a 2-quart casserole dish coated with non-stick vegetable spray. Bake, uncovered, at 350 degrees for one hour, or until hot and golden. Makes 4 servings.

A Lazy Susan is so handy for storing lots of jars and cans in the pantry. Give it a quick spin to bring the item you want right to the front of the cupboard.

Really Delicious Meatloaf

Lauren Webnar
Chino Valley, AZ

This recipe is a family favorite! Every person who tries it asks for the recipe, and it becomes their family favorite too. I often double the meatloaf ingredients and triple the sauce ingredients so we'll have plenty of leftovers for meatloaf sandwiches for lunch the next day! My family prefers it without the optional veggies added.

1 lb. ground beef
12 to 15 saltine crackers, crushed
1 egg, beaten
Optional: 1/2 onion, diced;
 1/2 green pepper, diced
1/4 c. catsup
3 T. brown sugar, packed
1 t. dry mustard
1/4 t. nutmeg

In a large bowl, mix together beef, crushed crackers and egg; add optional vegetables, if using. Set aside. In another bowl, mix together remaining ingredients; add 3/4 of catsup mixture to beef mixture. Shape beef into a loaf shape; place in an ungreased 9"x5" loaf pan or one-quart casserole dish. Spread remaining catsup mixture on top. Bake, uncovered, at 350 degrees for 45 minutes to one hour, until done and no longer pink in the center. Serves 4 to 6.

Mix up a meatloaf...no muss, no fuss. Combine all the ingredients in a large plastic zipping bag. Seal the bag and squish it until everything is well combined, then just toss the empty bag!

Ground Beef & Wild Rice Stroganoff

Bootsie Dominick
Suches, GA

This is an easy dish and it's delicious over the wild rice. It is different from the usual stroganoff. My husband really likes it!

6-oz. pkg. long-grain & wild rice mix, uncooked
1 lb. ground beef
3/4 c. onion, chopped
8-oz. pkg. sliced mushrooms
10-3/4 oz. can cream of mushroom soup
1 c. water
8-oz. container sour cream

Cook rice according to package directions. Meanwhile, in a large skillet over medium-high heat, cook beef with onion and mushrooms until beef is browned and crumbly; drain. Stir together mushroom soup and water in a bowl; add to beef mixture. Simmer over low heat for about 10 minutes. Stir in sour cream; cook another 5 minutes, or until heated through. Serve over cooked rice. Makes 6 servings.

A pat of herb butter makes warm dinner rolls extra scrumptious. Blend 1/2 cup softened butter with a teaspoon each of chopped fresh parsley, dill and chives. Roll into a log or pack into a crock... keep refrigerated to enjoy anytime.

The Mac & Cheese Everyone Likes

Jackie Bakunas
Forest Hill, MD

In our family, adults and kids don't always agree on what is "good" mac & cheese. I came up with this recipe to delight both the grown-ups and the kiddos. Now everyone asks for the mac & cheese "everyone likes," hence the name! I recommend shredding your own cheese for the best results. You can also add bread crumbs to the top before baking, if you like. Enjoy!

7 T. butter, sliced and divided
16-oz. pkg. elbow macaroni, uncooked
12-oz. can evaporated milk
1 c. plus 2 T. whole milk
3 eggs, beaten
1-1/2 t. salt
1/2 t. pepper
1 c. pasteurized process cheese, diced
3 c. shredded sharp Cheddar cheese, divided
2-1/2 c. shredded mild Cheddar cheese

Coat a 13"x9" glass baking pan with one tablespoon butter; set aside. Cook macaroni according to package directions, just until tender; drain and place in a very large bowl. Add remaining butter to hot macaroni; stir well. Add milks and eggs; stir well. Add salt, pepper, diced cheese and shredded cheeses, reserving some shredded cheese to sprinkle on top. Stir well and spread in pan. Sprinkle reserved cheese on top. Bake, uncovered, at 425 degrees for 35 to 40 minutes, until hot and bubbly. Makes 10 to 12 servings.

Prefer to shred cheese yourself? Freeze the wrapped block of cheese for 15 minutes...it will just glide across the grater! An 8-ounce package of shredded cheese equals 2 cups.

Can't-Miss
COMFORT FOOD MEALS

Oh-So-Good Chimichangas

Beckie Apple
Grannis, AR

I used to make this easy no-fuss crockpot meal before I retired because it was so nice to come home to for dinner. I have now been retired for several years and I still make it, because it's perfect on busy days. Enjoy with a chopped salad for a delicious meal.

8 frozen beef & cheese beef chimichangas
15-oz. can beef chili, with or without beans
16-oz. jar chunky salsa
8-oz. pkg. shredded Cheddar cheese
8-oz. container sour cream
3 green onions, diced

Line a 5-quart crockpot with a disposable plastic liner. Arrange frozen chimichangas in crockpot; top with chili and salsa. Sprinkle with shredded cheese; spoon sour cream on top and sprinkle with onions. Cover and cook on high setting for 4 hours. Serves 4 to 6.

Country-Style Barbecue Pork Ribs

Karen Valenti
Kansas City, KS

This crockpot recipe is so easy and only takes three ingredients! These ribs are delicious any time of year...I like to pair them with corn on the cob and baked beans. This is one of my family's favorite meals! I always use a plastic crock liner to save on clean-up.

2 lbs. country-style pork ribs
1 yellow onion, sliced
1-1/2 c. favorite barbecue sauce

In a 5-quart slow cooker, layer ribs, onion and sauce in order listed. Cover and cook on high setting for 6 hours, or on low setting for 8 hours. Makes 4 servings.

A smiling face is half the meal.
– Latvian proverb

Hobo Hawaiian Chicken Packets

Denise Ward
Coldwater, MI

After spending a day on the lake, this is a simple, delicious recipe for a summer evening. Spicy barbecue sauce can be used to add a little heat! I like to use red, yellow, orange and green peppers from the farmers' market.

1 c. favorite barbecue sauce
2 T. soy sauce
salt and pepper to taste
4 chicken breasts
4 slices canned pineapple
2 assorted peppers, diced

In a small bowl, stir together sauces, salt and pepper; set aside. Coat 4 large pieces of heavy-duty aluminum foil with non-stick vegetable spray. Top each piece of foil with a chicken breast and a pineapple slice; divide peppers evenly among the 4 foil pieces. Drizzle each with 1/4 cup sauce mixture; fold up the sides of foil to make a packet. Place packets on a hot grill. Cook for 20 to 25 minutes, turning halfway through cooking time, until chicken juices run clear when pierced. Packets may also be baked in the oven at 425 degrees for 30 to 35 minutes. Makes 4 servings.

Stem and seed green peppers in a flash! Hold the pepper upright on a cutting board, and use a sharp knife to slice each of the sides from the pepper. You'll then have 4 large pieces ready to slice or chop.

Easy Oven-Barbecued Chicken

Kathy Grashoff
Fort Wayne, IN

I love using my backyard grill, but when winter sets in here in the good old midwest, barbecuing goes indoors. I have really learned to use the broiler to achieve delicious chicken, burgers and steaks!

1 T. kosher salt
1 T. coarse pepper
8 to 10 chicken pieces
1 onion, sliced
2 c. favorite barbecue sauce

Combine salt and pepper; rub into all chicken pieces. Arrange chicken in a lightly greased shallow 13"x9" baking pan; arrange onion slices on top. Bake, uncovered, at 425 degrees for 10 minutes. Reduce oven temperature to 350 degrees; continue baking for 30 minutes. Brush barbecue sauce over chicken; bake for 10 minutes more. Turn over chicken; brush with sauce and bake another 10 minutes. Brush sauce over chicken again; broil skin-side up on high for 2 to 3 minutes, until golden. Serves 4 to 5.

Buttery sweet corn is so delicious...why not enjoy it more often? Melt 3 tablespoons butter in a microwave-safe dish; add 4 ears corn and roll to coat. Cover with plastic wrap and microwave on high for 6 to 8 minutes.

Steak & Potato Supper

Monty Rae Miles
Medford, OR

One of my daughter Jennifer's favorite meals. We enjoy this with steamed fresh green beans.

1-1/2 lbs. beef round steak, cut into serving-size pieces
1/3 c. all-purpose flour
1/4 c. oil
2 to 3 russet potatoes, peeled and cut in half
1/2 c. onion, chopped
1/2 t. salt
1/8 t. pepper
2 8-oz. cans tomato sauce

Dredge steak pieces in flour; set aside. Heat oil in a large skillet over medium-high heat. Working in batches, add steak and brown well on both sides; drain. Transfer steak to a greased 2-quart casserole dish. Arrange potatoes around steak; set aside. Drain skillet, scraping up any browned bits and adding to steak. Sprinkle onion, salt and pepper over all; cover with tomato sauce. Bake, covered, at 350 degrees for 1-1/2 hours, or until steak and potatoes are tender. Makes 4 servings.

Mom's Swiss Steak

Kimberly Redeker
Savoy, IL

This is one recipe I always ask for when coming home to Mom's house. It's a simple, wholesome meal that just tastes like home... it's great with mashed potatoes!

4 beef cube steaks
1/2 c. all-purpose flour
salt and pepper to taste
1/4 c. oil
10-3/4 oz. can cream of mushroom soup

Coat steaks in flour. Season with salt and pepper; set aside. Heat oil in a skillet over medium-high heat. Add steaks to skillet; cook until browned and crisp on edges. Flip and cook until crisp on other side. Transfer to a greased 13"x9" baking pan; spoon mushroom soup over steaks. Cover and bake at 350 degrees for one hour. Serves 4.

Easy Chicken & Dumplings

Cheran Lockerby
Richmond, VA

So easy and quick...real old-fashioned comfort food.

1 deli rotisserie chicken
1/2 c. butter, melted
salt and pepper to taste
1 c. milk
1 c. self-rising flour
2 c. chicken broth
10-3/4 oz. can cream of chicken soup

Pull or shred chicken, discarding skin and bones. Spread chicken in a lightly greased 13"x9" baking pan. Drizzle evenly with melted butter; season with salt and pepper. In a bowl, whisk together milk and flour. Pour slowly over chicken; do not stir. In the same bowl, whisk together chicken broth and chicken soup. Pour slowly over chicken; do not stir. (Dumplings will form while baking.) Bake, uncovered, at 375 degrees for 45 minutes. Let stand for 5 minutes for dumplings to finish forming; the longer it stands, the more dumplings. Makes 6 servings.

No self-rising flour in the cupboard? For each cup needed, substitute one cup all-purpose flour plus 1-1/2 teaspoons baking powder and 1/2 teaspoon salt. Simple!

Barbecued Franks & Noodles

Peggy Safarik
Conway, SC

This is a quick, easy and very economical recipe that my mother began making for her family of four, just after World War 2. She passed it along to me, and over the years I've gotten many requests for it from others, who just had to have the recipe! It's so very good and evokes fond memories of my childhood every time I prepare it.

1/4 c. canola oil
1/4 c. onion, chopped
12-oz. bottle chili sauce
1 T. Worcestershire sauce
3/4 c. water
1 T. light brown sugar, packed
16-oz. pkg. extra broad egg noodles, uncooked
16-oz. pkg. hot dogs

Combine oil and onion in a saucepan over low heat. Cook for about 10 minutes, stirring often. Stir in sauces, water and brown sugar. Simmer for 15 minutes, stirring occasionally. Meanwhile, cook noodles according to package directions. Drain and turn into a lightly greased shallow 13"x9" baking pan. Arrange hot dogs over noodles in pan. Spoon sauce mixture over hot dogs and noodles. Bake, uncovered, at 375 degrees for 30 minutes, or until bubbly and golden. Serves 6 to 8.

Food for friends doesn't have to be fancy. Your guests will be delighted with comfort foods like Grandma used to make. Invite them to help themselves from large platters set right on the table...so cozy!

Dump Hotdish

Joanne Mauseth
Clear Lake, SD

This is one of the first dishes Mom taught us to make when we were little. Growing up in a family with eight kids, it was fast, easy and everyone liked it. It was simple enough that all the beginner cooks made it when it was their turn to make supper. It never had any name other than "hotdish" when we were growing up. If you are cooking for a crowd, just double everything.

- 16-oz. pkg. wide egg noodles, uncooked
- 1 lb. ground beef
- 1/4 c. onion
- 10-3/4 oz. can cream of mushroom soup
- 10-3/4 oz. can tomato soup
- 15-1/2 oz. can kidney beans, drained
- 15-oz. can mixed vegetables, drained
- salt and pepper to taste

Cook noodles according to package directions; drain. Meanwhile, brown beef with onion in a skillet over medium heat; drain. Add cooked noodles and remaining ingredients to skillet; mix well. Transfer mixture to a buttered 3-quart casserole dish. Bake, uncovered, at 350 degrees for 20 to 30 minutes, until hot and bubbly. Makes 6 servings.

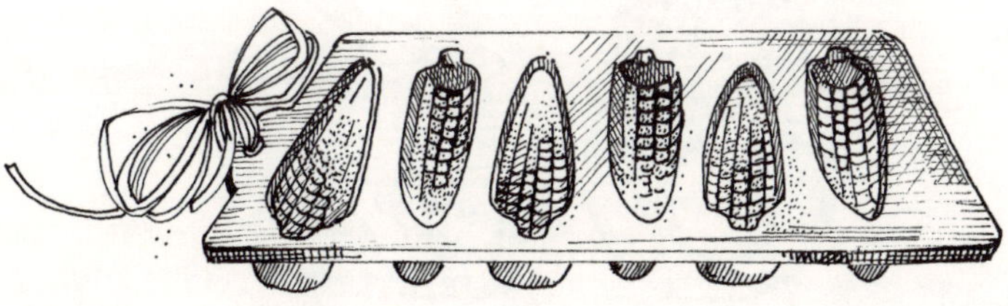

The kids will love eating "ears" of cornbread... just spoon the batter into a corn-shaped cast-iron baking pan.

Creamy Baked Chicken & Stuffing

Leona Krivda
Belle Vernon, PA

This is one of those recipes that's so easy, you can't believe it! It is a great dish for family or company, and so simple in a crockpot.

8 boneless, skinless chicken breasts
salt and pepper to taste
10-3/4 oz. can cream of chicken soup
1/4 c. water
1 c. herb-seasoned stuffing, crushed
1/4 c. butter, melted
8 slices white American cheese

Season all chicken breasts lightly with salt and pepper. Layer 4 chicken breasts in a lightly greased 5-quart crockpot; set aside. In a bowl, whisk together chicken soup and water; spoon half of mixture over chicken in crock. Repeat layering with remaining chicken and soup mixture. Sprinkle stuffing crumbs on top; drizzle melted butter over all. Cover and cook on high setting for 4 hours, or until chicken is tender. Arrange cheese slices on top; cover and cook another 30 minutes. Makes 8 servings.

Whip up a crock of honey butter to serve with warm biscuits at dinner. Simply blend one cup honey, one cup softened butter and one teaspoon vanilla extract. Store in a small crock.

Jam Chicken

Leslie Kirzner
Boonton, NJ

I like to rummage through my pantry to make up recipes. This recipe lends itself to that! You can doctor it up so easily...top the chicken with anything else you want, like the kitchen sink!

12-oz. jar strawberry, apricot or other favorite jam
4 bone-in or boneless chicken breasts
1 c. honey mustard
1/2 c. canned French fried onions
1 c. banana peppers, with liquid
2 T. balsamic vinegar
2 T. red wine or fruit juice

Spread a thick layer of jam in the bottom of a lightly greased 13"x9" baking pan. Arrange chicken pieces on top; spread mustard over chicken. Top with onions and banana peppers with liquid; drizzle with vinegar and wine or juice. Bake, uncovered, at 350 degrees for one hour, or until chicken juices run clear. Makes 4 servings.

Take it easy on alternate Fridays...arrange for a friendly dinner swap! One week, you make a double batch of a favorite casserole and deliver one to a friend. Next week, she returns the favor. You're sure to discover some great new recipes while gaining a little free time too.

Texas BBQ Chicken

Tammy Navarro
Littleton, CO

This is a delicious, easy way to make sweet, tender chicken in your crockpot. We like to shred the chicken and serve it on hamburger buns.

2 lbs. boneless, skinless chicken breasts
1/2 t. onion powder
1/4 t. garlic powder
salt and pepper to taste
2 c. favorite barbecue sauce
1-1/2 c. spiced cherry soda (not diet)
Optional: 6 hamburger buns, split

Place chicken in a 4-quart crockpot, sprinkling with seasonings as you layer. In a bowl, mix together barbecue sauce and soda; spoon over chicken. Cover and cook on high setting for 4 to 5 hours, or on low setting for 6 to 7 hours, until chicken is very tender. Shred chicken; stir back into mixture in crock. Serve spooned onto buns, if desired. Makes 6 servings.

Declare a picnic night at home! Just toss a checkered tablecloth on the dinner table and set out paper plates and disposable plastic utensils. Relax and enjoy dinner...no dishes to wash!

Bobbie's Beef Sandwiches

Becky Myers
Ashland, OH

This is a recipe from my dear sister-in-law Bobbie. She is an excellent cook and the most caring and thoughtful person you would ever want to meet. This is an easy recipe to prepare ahead and makes at least 12 large sandwiches. If you want to make this recipe gluten-free, simply use Worcestershire sauce instead of soy sauce.

3 lbs. beef chuck roast or stew stew beef, cut into chunks
5 to 6 stalks celery, chopped
3 onions, chopped
1/3 c. less-sodium soy sauce
12 sandwich buns, split

Combine all ingredients in a large roaster. Cover and bake at 325 degrees for at least 3 hours, until beef can be shredded with a fork. (May take longer depending on beef used.) Uncover; continue baking until some of the liquid cooks down. Stir beef into liquid in roaster. Spoon into sandwich buns and serve. May also be cooked in a 6-quart slow cooker on low setting for 8 to 10 hours. Makes 12 or more servings.

When burgers and hot dogs are on the menu, set up a topping bar with bowls of shredded cheese, crispy bacon, condiments and other tasty stuff. Everyone can just help themselves to their favorites.

Camp Neibel Hamburgers

James Rupert
White Bear Lake, MN

I learned this recipe 70 years ago, and I still enjoy it. I've taught it to my kids, and they love it too. Dill pickle spears and ruffled potato chips make a fine go-with.

1 lb. ground beef
1 to 2 T. oil
14-1/2 oz. can petite diced tomatoes, drained
14-3/4 oz. can cream-style corn
garlic salt or powder to taste

Divide beef into 4 patties. Cook patties in oil in a skillet until almost done; drain. Add tomatoes, corn and garlic salt or powder to skillet; stir well and heat through. Serve hot, dividing tomato mixture from skillet equally among the 4 patties. Makes 4 servings.

Pick up a stack of vintage plastic burger baskets. Lined with red-checked paper napkins, they're such fun for serving hot dogs, burgers and fries...clean-up is a snap too. Don't forget the pickle!

Can't-Miss COMFORT FOOD MEALS

Grandkids' Favorite Pizza Dogs

Carolyn Deckard
Bedford, IN

My great-grandkids came up with this recipe for fun, when staying for a sleepover. Now it's their favorite meal when we pick them up after school. Just add some chips and fresh fruit or veggies.

1/2 c. pizza sauce
8 hot dogs
8 hot dog buns, split
1 c. shredded mozzarella cheese

Add pizza sauce to a microwave-safe bowl; cover bowl with wax paper. Microwave on high for 30 to 45 seconds until hot; cover to keep warm. Place 4 hot dogs on a microwave-safe plate lined with a paper towel. Pierce hot dogs several times with fork. Cover with a paper towel. Microwave on high for one minute and 10 to 30 seconds, until heated through. Let stand 3 minutes. Repeat with remaining hot dogs. Serve hot dogs on buns, topped with warm pizza sauce and shredded cheese. Makes 8 servings.

Bobbie's Versatile Shredded Chicken

Bootsie Dominick
Suches, GA

Easy in a crockpot! This shredded chicken is really good as a sandwich or in a tortilla.

3 boneless, skinless chicken breasts
1-oz. pkg. ranch salad dressing mix
8-oz. pkg. cream cheese, unwrapped
6 sandwich buns, split, or tortillas
Garnish: crumbled bacon, shredded cheese, sliced green onions

Layer chicken breasts in a 4-quart crockpot; sprinkle with ranch dressing mix. Lay block of cream cheese on top. Cover and cook on low setting for 6 to 7 hours, until chicken is very tender. Shred chicken in crock; mix well with cream cheese. Serve on buns or tortillas, garnished as desired. Makes 6 servings.

Grandma's Sloppy Joes

Judy Schroff
Churubusco, IN

I came up with this recipe by making some changes to one I found in an old church cookbook. I think these are the best Sloppy Joes I've ever tasted and my family agrees. I hope you do too!

1 lb. ground beef
1/2 onion, diced
1 c. catsup
1/4 c. sugar
1/4 c. vinegar
2 T. Worcestershire sauce
Optional: soft bread crumbs
4 to 6 hamburger buns, split

Brown beef with onion in a skillet over medium heat; drain. Mix together catsup, sugar, vinegar and Worcestershire sauce in a small bowl; add to beef mixture in skillet and stir well. Bring to a boil; reduce heat to medium-low and simmer for 15 minutes. (If mixture is too liquid, add some bread crumbs to absorb the moisture.) Spoon mixture into buns and serve. Makes 4 to 6 servings.

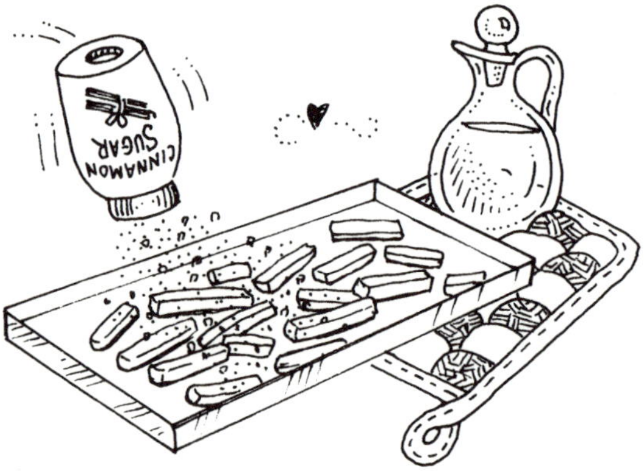

Sweet potato fries are deliciously different! Slice sweet potatoes into wedges, toss with olive oil and place on a baking sheet. Bake at 400 degrees for 20 to 30 minutes until tender, turning once. Sprinkle with a little cinnamon-sugar and serve warm.

SNACKS
for Special Days & Everyday

Southern Pimento Cheese

Beckie Apple
Grannis, AR

I grew up eating my Aunt Roxie's pimento cheese. So good! Now I make it myself, a little different than hers, but it's close. I like to make it for weekend snacks and of course, for our holiday side table. Enjoy with your favorite crispy crackers.

8-oz. pkg. finely shredded Cheddar cheese
2-oz. jar diced pimentos
3 T. mayonnaise
1 green onion, diced
1/2 t. spicy brown mustard
1/4 t. garlic powder
1/4 t. paprika

Combine cheese, pimentos with liquid and remaining ingredients in a bowl; stir until mixed well. Cover and chill for one to 2 hours before serving. Keep refrigerated. Makes 4 to 6 servings.

The secret to being a relaxed hostess...choose foods that can be prepared in advance. At party time, simply pull from the fridge and serve, or pop into a hot oven as needed.

SNACKS *for Special Days & Everyday*

Quickie Meatballs

Paula Marchesi
Auburn, PA

I always rely on these rich, tasty, cheesy meatballs for parties and unexpected guests. On busy weekends, I'll serve them alongside a tossed salad and garlic bread or rolls for a quick family meal.

3 c. finely shredded Cheddar or Monterey Jack cheese
1 c. biscuit baking mix
1/4 t. garlic powder
1/2 t. salt
1/4 t. pepper
1 lb. 90% lean ground beef

Combine all ingredients except beef in a large bowl; mix well. Crumble beef over mixture; mix well and shape into one-inch balls. Arrange meatballs in a lightly greased shallow 13"x9" baking pan. Bake, uncovered, at 400 degrees for 12 to 15 minutes, until beef is no longer pink; drain. Serve on a platter with toothpicks as an appetizer, or as desired for dinner. Makes about 4 dozen.

Making lots of meatballs? Grab a mini ice cream scoop or melon baller and start scooping...you'll be done in record time!

Pepperoni-Cheese Bread Sticks

Mel Chencharick
Julian, PA

Do some dipping with your favorite spaghetti sauce or pizza sauce! Great for watching your favorite team on a Sunday afternoon.

1 c. grated Parmesan cheese
2-3/4 c. biscuit baking mix
1 c. shredded Monterey Jack cheese
3-oz. pkg. sliced pepperoni, chopped
3/4 c. onion, finely chopped
1/2 c. sour cream
1/2 c. buttermilk
1 clove garlic, finely chopped

Add Parmesan cheese to a shallow bowl; set aside. Mix remaining ingredients in a large bowl until a dough forms. Drop dough by tablespoonfuls into Parmesan cheese; coat well and roll each into a 8-inch bread stick. Arrange bread sticks on 2 greased baking sheets, about 1-1/2 inches apart. Bake at 375 degrees for 15 to 18 minutes. Makes about 1-1/2 dozen.

Lemony iced tea is refreshing and party-perfect! Easy to double or triple for a crowd too. Add 9 teabags to 3 quarts boiling water. Let stand for 5 minutes, then discard teabags. Stir in a 12-ounce can of frozen lemonade concentrate. Sweeten to taste and serve over ice.

SNACKS *for Special Days & Everyday*

Easy Cheesy Bites

Melina Sarnese
Ontario, Canada

A wonderful and easy recipe to serve guests for your appetizer. A favorite in my family at Christmastime or anytime!

4 plain or whole-wheat English muffins, split and toasted
7-1/2 oz. container herbed chive & garlic cream cheese spread
2 T. shredded Gruyère cheese
2 T. shredded mozzarella cheese
2 T. grated Parmigiano Reggiano cheese

Spread cut sides of toasted muffins with cream cheese spread; sprinkle evenly with remaining cheeses. Arrange on a broiler pan. Broil for 5 minutes, or until cheese is melted and golden. Remove from oven; let stand for 5 minutes. Cut into quarters and serve. Makes about 2-1/2 dozen.

Puff Pastry Sausage Bites

Bootsie Dominick
Suches, GA

I love to make these when I have friends over...they go very fast.

1 lb. hot ground pork breakfast sausage
3/4 c. cream cheese, softened
17.3-oz. pkg. puff pastry, thawed

Set a baking sheet in oven at 400 degrees for a few minutes, until warmed. Meanwhile, brown and crumble sausage in a skillet over medium heat; drain. Add cream cheese; stir to mix well with sausage. Lay a sheet of puff pastry on warm baking sheet; spread with sausage mixture. Cover with remaining sheet of puff pastry; crimp edges with a fork. Bake at 400 degrees for 30 minutes. Cool slightly; cut into squares. Makes 1-1/2 to 2 dozen.

If someone volunteers to pitch in with get-together plans, or offers to bring a dish, let them...and be sure to return the favor!

Faux Rarebit Fondue

Louise Graybiel
Ontario, Canada

When I was a kid, old-fashioned Welsh rarebit was one of my favorite meals. I would even request it from my mom on my birthday. This is much quicker, since it uses soup and cheese spread to get it started. If you have leftovers, this tastes great reheated with steamed broccoli, on toasted English muffins or over poached eggs for breakfast.

2 10-3/4 oz. cans Cheddar cheese soup
1/2 c. evaporated milk
1/2 c. pasteurized process cheese sauce
1 t. Dijon mustard
1 T. Worcestershire sauce
1/2 t. hot pepper sauce
1/2 c. shredded sharp Cheddar cheese
pita wedges, pretzels, bread cubes, crostini, tortilla chips, cut-up vegetables

In a saucepan over medium-low heat, whisk together cheese soup and evaporated milk just until hot and bubbly. Stir in cheese sauce and mustard until melted and well combined. Turn heat to low; stir in Worcestershire sauce and hot sauce. Fold in Cheddar cheese; stir until just melted. Transfer to a fondue pot. Serve warm with desired dippers. Serves 8 to 10.

Keep party time simple. Serve one or 2 tried & true appetizers like cheese balls and dips, and pick up some tasty go-withs like pickles, marinated olives and cocktail nuts at the grocery store. Relax and enjoy your guests!

SNACKS *for Special Days & Everyday*

Pull-Apart Bacon-Garlic Bread

Laurie White
Geneseo, KS

I have made this tasty recipe several times. It is fun to add different ingredients for different flavors. Use your imagination!

1 lb. sliced hickory-smoked bacon
1 t. oil
3/4 c. green onions, chopped
3/4 c. green pepper, chopped
1 clove garlic, minced
3 7-1/2 oz. tubes refrigerated buttermilk biscuits, separated
1/2 c. margarine, melted
1/2 c. shredded Cheddar cheese

Cook bacon in a skillet over medium heat until crisp. Drain bacon on paper towels; crumble and set aside. Drain drippings from skillet. Add oil to skillet; heat over medium-high heat until oil is warm. Add onions, green pepper and garlic; sauté until vegetables are tender. Cut biscuits into quarters; place pieces in a large bowl. Add crumbled bacon, sautéed vegetables, margarine and cheese to bowl; toss until thoroughly mixed. Layer coated biscuit pieces in a 10" tube pan sprayed with non-stick vegetable spray. Bake at 350 degrees for 30 minutes, or until golden. Immediately turn out onto a large serving plate; serve warm. Makes 10 to 12 servings.

Big, colorful ice cubes for a party punch bowl...arrange thin slices of lemon and lime in muffin tins, fill with water and freeze.

Cuban Sliders

Tina Wright
Atlanta, GA

When we lived in Miami, Cuban sandwiches were a favorite in our family. These mini sandwiches are party-perfect! If you can't find roast pork at the deli, just double the ham.

12 slider buns, split
3 T. mustard
1/2 lb. deli baked ham, thinly sliced
1/2 lb. deli roast pork, thinly sliced
8 slices Swiss cheese
8-oz. jar pickle chips, drained
3 T. butter, melted
1 T. dried parsley
1-1/2 t. garlic powder
1-1/2 t. onion powder

Place bottom halves of buns in a 13"x9" baking pan sprayed with non-stick vegetable spray. Spread mustard onto buns. Layer ham evenly across buns, followed by roast pork, Swiss cheese and pickles. Add top halves of buns. In a cup, mix together melted butter and seasonings; brush over buns. Cover with aluminum foil. Bake at 350 degrees for 25 minutes; uncover. Return to oven for another 5 minutes, or until buns are golden. Let stand for a few minutes; cut apart sandwiches and serve. Makes 12 sandwiches.

Creamy Vegetable Dip

Judy Phelan
Macomb, IL

This dip is a big hit with my family! Serve it with crackers as a dip, or with bread as a sandwich spread.

8-oz. pkg. cream cheese, softened
1 T. mayonnaise
1 T. lemon juice
1/2 t. salt
1/8 t. pepper
3/4 c. carrot, peeled and grated
1/2 c. green pepper, diced
1/2 c. celery, diced
1/3 c. green onions, diced

In a large bowl, combine cream cheese, mayonnaise, lemon juice, salt and pepper. Beat with an electric mixer on medium speed until smooth; fold in vegetables using a spoon. Cover and chill for 2 to 3 hours before serving. Makes 16 servings.

SNACKS *for Special Days & Everyday*

Copycat Sliders

Sandy Coffey
Cincinnati, OH

From our favorite burger place! Great flavor, loved by the whole family for years. These can be served for lunch or as a fun appetizer.

2/3 c. onion, finely chopped
1 lb. ground beef chuck
1/4 c. dry bread crumbs
2 eggs, beaten
1 t. pepper
Optional: 8 to 12 slices American cheese
8 to 10 dinner rolls, split

Spread onion evenly in an ungreased 13"x9" baking pan; set aside. In a large bowl, mix beef, bread crumbs, eggs and pepper. Spoon mixture evenly over onion in pan. With a drinking straw, poke holes closely and evenly over beef mixture. Bake, uncovered, at 400 degrees for about 20 minutes, until beef is no longer pink. Remove from oven. If desired, top with cheese slices; return to oven for one to 2 minutes, until cheese is melted. Cut into squares and serve on dinner rolls. Makes 8 to 10 sandwiches.

Tropical Tea

Barb Bargdill
Gooseberry Patch

The perfect beverage for sipping on a hot summer day!

12-oz. can frozen pineapple-orange juice concentrate
4 c. homemade or bottled iced tea
4-1/2 c. water
ice cubes or crushed ice

In a large pitcher, combine juice concentrate, iced tea and water; mix well. Cover and chill; serve over ice. Makes 12 servings.

Just for fun, serve frosty beverages in pint-size Mason jars.

French Bread Pizza

Ann Farris
Biscoe, AR

This is so easy to make, and you can add or subtract any ingredients as your family prefers. Serve as an appetizer, or as a simple meal with a green salad on the side.

1 loaf French bread, halved lengthwise
1 T. butter, melted
2 cloves garlic, minced
1 c. marinara or pizza sauce
2 c. shredded mozzarella cheese, divided
3-oz. pkg. pepperoni slices
2 T. grated Parmesan cheese
4-oz. can sliced mushrooms, drained
1/2 green pepper, diced
1/2 c. onion, diced

Place bread halves on an ungreased baking sheet, cut-side up. Mix together melted butter and garlic; brush over bread. Bake at 400 degrees for 10 minutes, or until lightly toasted. Remove from oven; spread with marinara or pizza sauce. Top with 1-1/2 cups mozzarella cheese and remaining ingredients; sprinkle with remaining mozzarella cheese. Bake at 400 degrees for 10 minutes, or until cheese is melted. Slice and serve. Makes 5 servings.

Have appetizers for dinner! Set up a family-size sampler with French Bread Pizza, mini egg rolls, potato skins and a bunch of dippers to try too. Don't forget the French fries!

SNACKS
for Special Days & Everyday

Parker's Pepperoni Roll-Ups

Parker Holsinger
Belpre, OH

I am an 11-year-old who likes to help make things in the kitchen. This is one of my favorite things to make. They're so good!

2 8-oz. tubes refrigerated crescent rolls
3-oz. pkg. pepperoni slices
8-oz. pkg. shredded mozzarella cheese
1 egg, beaten
1 t. garlic powder
1 t. dried oregano
1 t. dried basil
Garnish: shredded Parmesan cheese
Optional: warmed pizza sauce

Separate crescent rolls into triangles. Place at least 4 pepperoni slices down the center of each triangle; sprinkle with mozzarella cheese. Starting at the wide end, roll up each triangle to the narrow end. Arrange on an ungreased baking sheet. Brush with beaten egg; mix together seasonings and sprinkle over rolls. Bake at 375 degrees for 15 minutes, or until golden. Sprinkle with Parmesan cheese; serve with pizza sauce for dipping, if desired. Makes 16 servings.

Create a table runner...a quick way to make any meal more festive. Purchase cotton fabric in a cheerful seasonal or vintage print, hem or pink the edges and you're done!

Creamy Cheese Spread

Ramona Storm
Gardner, IL

I'm always on the lookout for simple, do-ahead recipes. This is a great make-ahead recipe to set out for your guests to snack on while you're putting the final touches on the holiday meal.

2 5-oz. jars pasteurized process cheese spread
8-oz. pkg. cream cheese, softened
1 T. Worcestershire sauce
garlic powder to taste
assorted crackers

Combine cheeses in a large bowl; beat with an electric mixer on medium speed until well blended. Add Worcestershire sauce and garlic powder; stir just until combined. Transfer to a serving bowl and cover with plastic wrap. Refrigerate for several hours or overnight. Serve with crackers. Makes 16 servings.

Holiday Ham Spread

Danielle Boyd
Wytheville, VA

This ham spread is a family favorite and is a great addition to any family gathering.

8-oz. pkg. cream cheese, softened
1-oz. pkg. ranch salad dressing mix
5-oz. can smoked ham, drained
favorite snack crackers

In a large bowl, mix together cream cheese and dressing mix; set aside. In a small bowl, flake ham with 2 forks; add to cheese mixture and stir until well combined. Cover and chill until serving time. Serve with crackers. Makes 8 servings.

Make it easy on guests...serve foods that can be eaten in one or 2 bites.

SNACKS *for Special Days & Everyday*

Grandpa Ed's Potato Chip Chicken Fingers

Gladys Kielar
Whitehouse, OH

These chicken fingers get their crunch from potato chips instead of deep-frying. Try this with a variety of chip flavors, from sour cream & chive to barbecue...they're all sure to be yummy!

2 boneless, skinless chicken breasts
6-oz. pkg. potato chips
1 egg, beaten
2 T. milk
Garnish: honey mustard dip, barbecue sauce, salsa or other sauce

Cut chicken into finger-size pieces; set aside. Add potato chips to a large plastic zipping bag; seal bag and crush chips. Whisk together egg and milk in a small bowl. Dip chicken pieces into egg mixture, then into crushed chips in bag. Arrange chicken on an ungreased baking sheet. Bake at 400 degrees for 20 minutes, or until chicken juices run clear when pierced, turning once while baking. Serve with your favorite dipping sauce. Serves 4 to 5.

Try serving "light" dippers with hearty full-flavored dips and spreads. Bite-size baby vegetables, pita wedges, baked tortilla chips and multi-grain crispbread are all sturdy enough to scoop, yet won't overshadow the flavor of the dip.

Cowboy Caviar

Karen Wilson
Defiance, OH

This tasty dip is an easy make-ahead appetizer for tailgating or entertaining friends. It's so simple to prepare and is always a hit with guests. Serve with your favorite tortilla chips.

2 15-1/2 oz. cans black beans, drained
2 c. frozen corn, thawed
2 to 3 ripe tomatoes, chopped
1 avocado, peeled, pitted and diced
1/2 c. red onion, chopped
1/4 c. fresh cilantro, chopped

Combine all ingredients in a bowl; mix gently. Pour Lime Dressing over mixture; toss to mix well. Cover and refrigerate. Stir again before serving. Makes 8 servings.

Lime Dressing:

1/4 c. lime juice
2 T. olive oil
1 T. red wine vinegar
1 t. salt
1/2 t. pepper

Combine all ingredients in a blender; process until well mixed.

Arrange a selection of finger foods on a vintage cutting board or tray for a fun party presentation.

SNACKS *for Special Days & Everyday*

Corn Dog Muffins

Angela Murphy
Tempe, AZ

My kids love to snack on these! Serve with catsup for dipping.

2 8-1/2 oz. pkgs. corn muffin mix
2 T. brown sugar, packed
2 eggs, beaten
1 c. milk
11-oz. can corn, drained
4 hot dogs, thinly sliced

In a bowl, combine corn muffin mix and brown sugar; mix well. In another bowl, whisk together eggs and milk; add to muffin mixture and stir until moistened. Batter will be thin. Fold in corn and hot dogs. Spoon batter into well-greased muffin cups, filling 3/4 full. Bake at 400 degrees for 14 to 18 minutes, until golden. Serve warm. Makes about 1-1/2 dozen.

Pick up a set of stackable silicone baking cups in fun colors. So handy for baking muffins...perfect for serving mini portions of fruit, nuts or chips too!

Shredded Beef Cheese Ball

Karen Suvak
Galena, OH

This is a family favorite at gatherings, especially for the holidays. When chopping the beef, I use a mini food processor or a food chopper to chop very fine. Serve with crackers.

2 8-oz. pkgs. cream cheese, softened
2 t. sweet onion, chopped
1/4 c. mayonnaise
4 t. mustard
5 2-1/2 oz. pkgs. sliced beef, finely chopped and divided

Combine all ingredients in a bowl, reserving half of the chopped beef. Mix with your hands; form into a ball. Pat the reserved beef all around outside of ball. Wrap in plastic wrap; refrigerate until serving time. Serves 12 to 15.

Hot Spiced Cranberry Cider

Carolyn Deckard
Bedford, IN

My family's favorite cider for our Christmas open house every year. It goes well with a platter of homemade cookies and breads.

8 c. apple cider
6 c. cranberry juice cocktail
1/4 c. brown sugar, packed
4 4-inch cinnamon sticks
1-1/2 t. whole cloves
1 orange, thinly sliced

Combine all ingredients in a very large saucepan. Bring to a boil over high heat. Reduce heat to low; simmer for 15 to 20 minutes to blend flavors. With a slotted spoon, remove cinnamon sticks, cloves and orange slices. Ladle hot cider into mugs and serve. Serves 24.

Constant use will not wear ragged the fabric of friendship.
– Dorothy Parker

SNACKS
for Special Days & Everyday

Hot Spicy Chicken Dip

Sophia Collins
McHenry, MS

This dip was always a regular at our Christmas Eve parties and was the first appetizer to go! I hope you'll love it too.

2 12-oz. cans chicken breast, drained
8-oz. pkg. cream cheese, softened
14-oz. bottle ranch salad dressing
5-oz. bottle hot pepper sauce
tortilla chips

Add chicken to a bowl; flake into smaller pieces. Add cream cheese, salad dressing and hot sauce. Beat with an electric mixer on medium speed until well blended. Transfer mixture to a lightly greased 2-quart casserole dish. Bake, uncovered, at 350 degrees for 30 minutes. Let cool for 10 to 15 minutes. Serve warm with tortilla chips. Makes 12 servings.

Hot Artichoke Dip

Crystal Shook
Catawba, NC

This yummy dip is great to take to parties, so simple and easy. Serve with your favorite pita chips or crunchy pretzels.

2 14-1/2 oz. cans artichoke hearts in water, drained and chopped
1 c. grated Parmesan cheese
1 c. mayonnaise
1 t. garlic powder
1/4 t. Worcestershire sauce

Combine all ingredients in a bowl; mix well. Spread mixture in a one-quart casserole dish sprayed with non-stick vegetable spray. Bake, uncovered, at 350 degrees for 20 to 25 minutes, until heated through. Serves 6 to 8.

For a super-quick appetizer, set a softened block of cream cheese on a serving plate and spoon salsa over it. Serve with tortilla chips.

Quick & Easy Candied Dill Pickles

Eileen Bennett
Jenison, MI

In 1992, I took this recipe from the Arkansas cookbook on my kitchen shelf. I probably picked up this cookbook on a trip to Branson, Missouri with a day trip to Eureka Springs, Arkansas. These pickles are on every holiday menu. My granddaughter Tara loves these so much, she sent me 6 bottles of tarragon vinegar so I would always have the ingredients on hand for the pickles! We triple the recipe and never have any leftovers.

2 24-oz. jars dill pickle spears or slices (no garlic)
1/2 c. tarragon vinegar
2-3/4 c. sugar
2 t. pickling spices

Drain pickles, adding juice to a large bowl. Combine juice with vinegar and sugar; whisk to blend until sugar is dissolved. Add pickles to bowl; enclose spices in a small cheesecloth bag and add to bowl. Let stand at room temperature for 4 hours. Cover and refrigerate for 4 days before serving. If there are any pickles left to store after first serving, remove spice bag after one week. Makes about one quart.

Show off colorful vegetable salads and pickles by serving them in big one-gallon canning or pickle jars. Just wrap each jar in a napkin or tea towel to protect them on the way to a potluck or picnic.

SNACKS
for Special Days & Everyday

Pickled Onions

Roberta Simpkins
Mentor on the Lake, OH

I always have a jar of these delicious onions on hand in my refrigerator. We put them on everything from eggs to tacos!

2 to 3 medium red onions, sliced
Optional: 2 jalapeño peppers, sliced
3 to 4 cloves garlic, minced
1-1/2 c. white vinegar
1/2 c. water
1 T. whole peppercorns
1 T. sugar
1 T. salt
1 to 2 pint-size canning jars with lids, sterilized

Layer onions, jalapeño peppers if using and garlic in one to 2 canning jars; set aside. In a large saucepan, combine vinegar, water, peppercorns, sugar and salt. Cook and stir over medium heat until sugar and salt are dissolved. Bring to a boil; immediately pour over mixture in jars. Press with a spoon to make sure onions are covered with liquid. Add jar lids; let stand on the counter until cooled to room temperature. Refrigerate once cooled. Makes about one quart.

Whip up a tasty pizza with whatever you have on hand! Top a ready-to-bake pizza crust with pizza sauce, sliced baked chicken or grilled steak and fresh or cooked veggies. Finish with a sprinkle of cheese and bake until hot and bubbly, about 10 minutes at 400 degrees. Yummy!

Fried Corn Nuggets

Kay Turner
Dothan, AL

These are a favorite here in lower Alabama...we enjoy them often. Make as many or as few at a time as you like. Try dipping them in ranch dressing...yummy!

15-1/4 oz. can corn
14-3/4 oz. can creamed corn
1/2 c. yellow cornmeal
1/2 c. all-purpose flour
1 egg
2 T. milk
salt and pepper to taste
1/8 t. nutmeg
oil for frying

Combine both cans of corn in a bowl; mix well and spoon into an ice cube tray. Freeze. When ready to fry, combine remaining ingredients except oil in a bowl; mix well. Add several inches oil to a large saucepan; heat over medium-high heat to 350 degrees. Turn corn nuggets out of ice cube tray. Dip each nugget into batter and add to saucepan, a few at a time. Cook just until nuggets are golden. Drain on paper towels. Makes about 2-1/2 dozen.

For a quick & easy snack that everybody loves, nothing beats a big bowl of popcorn. Jazz it up with a sprinkle of grated Parmesan cheese or taco seasoning, or serve it the classic way, with butter and salt.

SNACKS *for Special Days & Everyday*

Zippy Salsa

Lisa Staib
Tumbling Shoals, AR

This salsa comes together in minutes and has a different zing to it. Wonderful with any kind of chip...corn, blue corn, tortilla. Wonderful pre-game, tailgate, appetizer or over chicken nachos!

10-oz. can red enchilada sauce
1 giant ripe tomato, diced
1/2 c. pepperoncini peppers, diced and drained
1/4 c. onion, diced
2 T. lime juice
1 t dried oregano

Mix all ingredients well in a large bowl; transfer to a canning jar or other covered container. Chill for several hours; shake before serving. Makes 8 to 12 servings.

Strawberry Lemonade Smoothie

Carrie Kelderman
Pella, IA

This is a wonderfully refreshing smoothie to be enjoyed on a warm summer day! Our family loves to sit on our deck and sip on this as we scan the Iowa countryside behind our home.

2 c. homemade or bottled lemonade
6-oz. container lemon yogurt
2 c. frozen unsweetened sliced strawberries
1/2 t. vanilla extract

Combine all ingredients in a blender; cover and process until well blended. Serve immediately. Makes 4 servings.

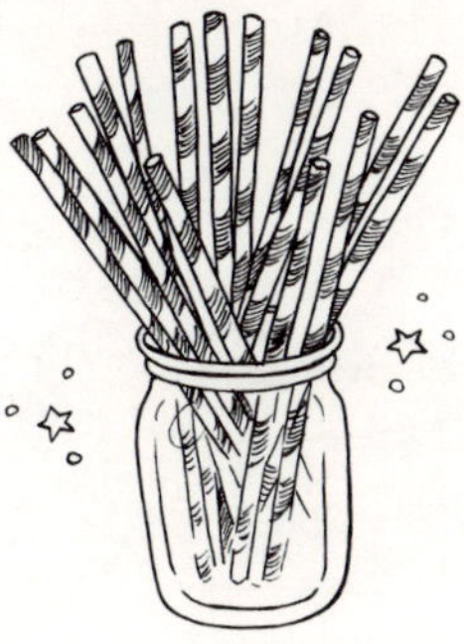

Striped drinking straws make any occasion a party in a jiffy!

Super-Simple COMFORT FOODS

Crispy Baked Chicken Wings

Robin Hill
Rochester, NY

No muss, no fuss...we love these for casual meals and parties. Serve with ranch dressing and celery sticks. Yummy!

4 lbs. chicken wings
1/2 c. butter
2 cloves garlic, minced
1 c. grated Parmesan cheese
1 T. dried parsley
1 T. dried oregano
2 t. paprika
1/2 t. salt
1/2 t. pepper

Separate chicken wings, discarding tips; set aside. Combine butter and garlic in a small saucepan over low heat; cook for 3 to 5 minutes, until butter is melted and garlic is fragrant. Combine cheese and seasonings in a shallow bowl. Dip chicken wings into butter mixture; coat lightly with cheese mixture. Arrange wings on a lightly greased broiler pan. Drizzle with any remaining butter. Bake, uncovered, at 350 degrees for about one hour, until golden and chicken juices run clear when pierced. Serves 8 to 10.

Jolly Dipping Sauce

Julie Perkins
Anderson, IN

Yummy with party franks, meatballs and chicken nuggets.

1 c. catsup
2/3 c. orange juice
1/4 c. brown sugar, packed

Combine all ingredients in a small saucepan. Cook and stir over medium heat until brown sugar dissolves. Serve warm. Makes about 2 cups.

A festive container for chips in a jiffy! Simply tie a knot in each corner of a bright-colored bandanna and tuck a bowl into the center.

Kitty's Hot Chicken Sandwiches

Tammy Navarro
Littleton, CO

This is an easy recipe to put together when you are in a hurry. You can use rotisserie chicken or cooked chicken breasts...it's a very good way to use leftover chicken. Enjoy!

2 c. cooked chicken, cubed or shredded
1 c. pasteurized process cheese, cubed
1 stalk celery, diced
1/3 c. mayonnaise
salt and pepper to taste
6 hamburger buns or 12 slider buns, toasted and buttered

In a greased 1-1/2 quart casserole dish, combine all ingredients except buns. Stir until well combined. Bake, covered, at 450 degrees for 35 to 45 minutes, stirring occasionally, until heated through and celery is tender. To serve, spoon chicken mixture onto buttered, toasted buns. Serves 6.

Warm sandwich buns for a crowd...easy! Fill a roaster with buns, cover with heavy-duty aluminum foil and cut several slits in the foil. Top with several dampened paper towels and tightly cover with more foil. Bake at 250 degrees for 20 minutes. Rolls will be hot and steamy.

Fall-Off-the-Bone Pork Ribs

Donna Carter
Ontario, Canada

I received this recipe from a co-worker many years ago, and have been using it ever since. It's so easy to prepare and results in fall-off-the-bone ribs that are just delicious. I use pork back ribs only...they're easier to cut through the bone, more meaty and tastier. I double the ingredients according to how many packages of ribs I use so that the ribs are nice and saucy.

2 2-1/2 lb. pkgs. pork back ribs, cut into serving-size portions
2 10-1/2 oz. cans beef consommé
1/2 c. soy sauce
1/2 c. honey
garlic powder to taste

Arrange ribs in a greased large roasting pan; set aside. Combine remaining ingredients in a saucepan. Cook and stir over low heat until honey is melted; spoon over ribs in pan. Cover and bake at 325 degrees for 2-1/2 hours, or until very tender. Serves 8 to 12.

Fill a relish tray with crunchy baby carrots, cherry tomatoes, broccoli flowerets and a hollowed-out green pepper filled with ranch dressing for dipping...ready to serve in a jiffy!

SNACKS
for Special Days & Everyday

Most Favorite Stuffed Mushrooms

Kimberly Redeker
Savoy, IL

These stuffed mushrooms are the bomb! People who say they don't like mushrooms change their minds after tasting these. They're great with steak, and also great as an appetizer on their own.

8-oz. pkg. whole mushrooms, stems removed
3/4 c. panko bread crumbs
1/2 c. grated Parmesan cheese
2 t. dried thyme
1 t. garlic, minced
1/4 t. salt
1/4 t. pepper
1/4 c. butter, melted and divided

Arrange mushroom caps in a lightly greased 13"x9" baking pan or 10" cast-iron skillet; set aside. Toast panko crumbs in a skillet over medium-high heat until golden. Combine panko crumbs, cheese and seasonings in a bowl; add 2 tablespoons melted butter. Mix well and spoon into mushroom caps. Drizzle with remaining butter. Bake, uncovered, at 375 degrees for 15 minutes. Serves 4.

Spice up your favorite ranch dressing for dipping and salads! To one cup of ranch dressing, whisk in 1/4 teaspoon chili powder and 1/2 teaspoon ground cumin. Let stand for 5 minutes for flavors to blend.

Dill Pickle Topper

Valerie Sholes
Blaine, MN

This is a delicious condiment to top burgers, serve as a dip with chips or crackers or add to a salad dressing.

8-oz. pkg. light cream cheese, softened
1 t. Worcestershire sauce
1/4 c. dill pickle juice
1 T. fresh dill weed, snipped, or 1 t. dried dill weed
1/4 t. garlic powder
1/4 t. onion powder
4 whole dill pickles, diced and drained
Optional: 3 slices bacon, crisply cooked and crumbled

In a bowl, mix together cream cheese, Worcestershire sauce and pickle juice to desired consistency. Stir in remaining ingredients. Cover and refrigerate for 30 minutes; serve as desired. Makes 8 servings.

Cheddar Cheese Sauce for Steak Fries

Teresa Verell
Roanoke, VA

This recipe is a family favorite...we just love it!

1 c. pasteurized process cheese sauce
2/3 c. shredded extra-sharp Cheddar cheese
1/4 c. evaporated milk
1/2 t. salt

Combine cheeses and evaporated milk in a small saucepan over medium-low heat. Cook, stirring often, until cheeses have melted and sauce is smooth. Stir in salt. Cover and keep warm until serving time. Serves 4.

The better part of one's life consists of one's friendships.
– Abraham Lincoln

SNACKS
for Special Days & Everyday

Avocado Ranch Dressing & Dip

Lisa Barger
Conroe, TX

This recipe is quick & easy and oh-so delicious. It's a favorite in my household and it will be in yours, too!

1/2 c. low-fat buttermilk
1/4 c. sour cream
3 T. mayonnaise
1 avocado, peeled, pitted and chopped
1 T. onion, minced
1 T. fresh cilantro, chopped
1 clove garlic, minced
2 t. lemon juice
1/2 t. hot pepper sauce
3/4 t. salt
1/4 t. pepper

Combine all ingredients in a food processor; pulse to combine. Process until smooth; transfer to a covered container. Keep refrigerated up to 3 days. Makes about 1-1/2 cups.

Sandy's Chip Dip

Sandy Ward
Anderson, IN

This is a nice change from the usual dips sold at the market. Try it out on game night and see the reviews come in for more! Serve with your favorite potato chips and fresh veggies.

24-oz. container small-curd cottage cheese
16-oz. jar mayonnaise
1-oz. pkg. ranch or buttermilk salad dressing mix

Combine all ingredients in a large bowl; mix well. Cover and chill for several hours before serving. Makes about 5 cups.

Colorful scooped-out peppers make fun containers for dips and sauces.

Hot Crab Cracker Dunk

Eileen Bennett
Jenison, MI

A Bennett family appetizer tradition! Served since the 1960s, it's a favorite recipe enjoyed by the kids as well as adults. Even our "don't like seafood" family & friends love this special holiday dish. Round buttery crackers are tasty with this dip.

2 8-oz. pkgs. cream cheese
3 4-1/2 oz. cans crabmeat, flaked
6 T. mayonnaise
3 T. white wine
4 t. mustard
1 t. sugar
2/3 t. onion juice
1/8 t. seasoned salt
garlic salt to taste

Mix together all ingredients in the top of a double boiler. Cook over medium heat until heated through, stirring occasionally. Transfer to a chafing dish or small crockpot to keep warm for serving. Makes 8 to 10 servings.

Hosting a get-together for family & friends? Serve nostalgic soft drinks like root beer, orange pop and grape fizz in glass bottles, just for fun!

SNACKS *for Special Days & Everyday*

The Best Secret Garlic Bread

Brenda Schlosser
Moore, OK

I first heard about this recipe from a Sacramento, California television personality. I usually triple the garlic spread ingredients and refrigerate some of it for future uses. Enjoy!

1 loaf French bread, halved lengthwise
1/3 c. mayonnaise
1/4 c. butter, softened
1/4 c. grated Parmesan cheese
1 T. Italian seasoning
2 or more cloves garlic, finely minced

Place bread halves on a parchment paper-lined baking sheet, cut-side up; set aside. Mix remaining ingredients together; spread mixture over both halves of bread. Broil until bubbly and golden. Slice and serve. Serves 8.

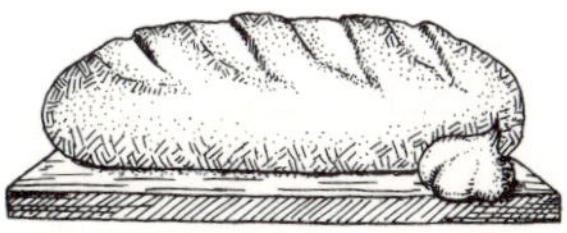

Jessica's Spinach Dip

Jessica Kraus
Delaware, OH

This is far and away my go-to dip for parties and potlucks. I am always asked for the recipe and always bring home an empty bowl. The longer it's in the fridge, the better it gets!

2 c. sour cream
1 c. mayonnaise
10-oz. pkg. frozen chopped spinach, thawed and squeezed dry
8-oz. can water chestnuts, drained and chopped
1 c. green onions, chopped
1 red pepper, chopped
1-oz. pkg. vegetable dip mix

Mix all ingredients in a large bowl. Cover and refrigerate for 8 hours or overnight before serving. Makes 10 servings.

Keep hot appetizers toasty until serving time in a 250-degree oven.

Amish Peanut Butter

Marsha Baker
Palm Harbor, FL

We used to live in Ohio near Amish country, where the restaurants always have this tasty topping on their tables, and sell it in their stores. I was thrilled to find this simple recipe to make it myself and love giving it as gifts.

2 c. brown sugar, packed
1 c. water
2 T. corn syrup
1 t. maple syrup
16-oz. jar creamy peanut butter
16-oz. jar marshmallow creme

In a large saucepan, combine brown sugar, water, corn syrup and maple syrup. Cook and stir over medium heat until mixture comes to a boil. Remove from heat; let cool for about 15 minutes. In a large bowl, combine peanut butter and marshmallow creme; stir until smooth and well blended. Gradually add cooled sugar mixture; stir until smooth and well combined. Transfer to covered containers; does not need to be refrigerated. Makes about 24 servings.

Easy Fruit Dip

Monica Britt
Fairdale, WV

This easy recipe has been a family favorite in our family for years. We serve it for showers, cookouts and luncheons with our favorite seasonal ripe fruits.

8-oz. pkg. cream cheese, softened
8-oz. jar marshmallow creme
1/2 c. sour cream

Combine all ingredients in a large bowl. Beat with an electric mixer on low to medium speed until well mixed. Cover and chill until serving time. Makes 12 servings.

Nestle a bowl of creamy dip inside a larger bowl filled with crushed ice to keep it fresh and tasty.

Easy-as-Pie DESSERTS

Ugly Duckling Cake

Leona Krivda
Belle Vernon, PA

A funny name for a really scrumptious cake! Serve it warm or cool, topped with ice cream or whipped cream if you like.

15-1/4 oz. pkg. yellow cake mix
15-1/4 oz. can fruit cocktail
2-1/3 c. flaked coconut, divided
2 eggs, beaten
1/2 c. brown sugar, packed
1/2 c. evaporated milk
1/2 c. butter
1/2 c. sugar

In a large bowl, combine dry cake mix, fruit cocktail with syrup, one cup coconut and eggs. Stir until blended; beat with an electric mixer on medium speed for 2 minutes. Pour batter into a greased and floured 13"x9" baking pan. Sprinkle with brown sugar. Bake at 325 degrees for 45 minutes, or until cake springs back when lightly touched. Remove from oven; set aside. In a small saucepan over medium heat, bring evaporated milk, butter and sugar to a boil. Boil for 2 minutes. Remove from heat; stir in remaining coconut. Spoon mixture over hot cake in pan; cut into squares. Makes 12 to 15 servings.

Making dessert for a crowd? It's tricky to successfully double or triple recipe ingredients for cakes or cookies. Instead, choose a recipe like Ugly Duckling Cake that feeds a bunch, or make several batches of a single recipe until you have the quantity you need.

Easy-as-Pie DESSERTS

Marie's Strawberry Shortcake

Jennie Gist
Gooseberry Patch

Just like Mom used to make! With five kids in the family, we had pretty simple meals and dessert was a special treat, when we had it. This is one Mom made fairly often in the summertime, when strawberries were plentiful.

4 c. fresh strawberries, hulled and sliced
1/4 c. plus 1/3 c. sugar, divided
2-1/3 c. biscuit baking mix
2/3 c. milk
3 T. butter, melted
Garnish: whipped cream

In a large bowl, toss together strawberries and 1/4 cup sugar; set aside. In another bowl, combine remaining sugar, baking mix, milk and melted butter. Stir until a soft dough forms. Spread dough in an ungreased 8" round cake pan. Bake at 425 degrees for 15 to 20 minutes, until golden. Turn out of pan; cut into wedges. Split wedges and fill with strawberries. Top with a dollop of whipped cream and serve. Makes 6 to 8 servings.

Fresh-picked berries are a special summer pleasure. Store them in a colander in the refrigerator to allow cold air to circulate around them. No need to rinse until you're ready to use them!

Pineapple Cheesecake Pie

Pam Lunn
Pensacola, FL

This creamy, no-bake pie is the perfect summer dessert. It is a staple at our home here in Florida when the temperatures are soaring outside. My husband loves how delicious it tastes, and I love how easy it is to prepare.

8-oz. pkg. cream cheese, softened
1/2 c. sugar
1 t. vanilla extract
20-oz. can crushed pineapple, drained
8-oz. container frozen whipped topping, thawed and divided
9-inch graham cracker crust
Optional: 1/4 c. toasted flaked coconut

In a large bowl, combine cream cheese, sugar and vanilla. Beat with an electric mixer on medium speed until smooth and creamy. Stir in pineapple with a spoon until well blended. Gently fold in half of whipped topping; spoon mixture into graham cracker crust. Top with remaining whipped topping, spreading to cover pie. Sprinkle with coconut, if using. Cover and refrigerate at least 4 to 5 hours before serving. Slice and serve. Store covered in the refrigerator. Makes 6 to 8 servings.

For best results when baking, preheat the oven first. Turn on the oven and set it to the correct temperature at least 15 minutes ahead of time.

Simple Apple Dessert Coffee Cake

Linda Smith
Fountain Hills, AZ

I love apples and love this recipe because it is simple and easy to make. It can be served as either a breakfast coffee cake or a dessert cake. Just the thing to take to potlucks and family gatherings!

7 to 8 Granny Smith apples, peeled, cored and sliced
2 c. all-purpose flour
2 c. sugar
2 t. baking powder
1 t. salt
2 eggs, beaten
1/2 c. butter, sliced or diced
cinnamon to taste
1 c. chopped pecans
Garnish: whipped cream or vanilla ice cream

Arrange apple slices evenly in the bottom of a lightly greased 13"x9" baking pan; set aside. In a large bowl, mix flour, sugar, baking powder and salt. Add eggs and stir well; mixture will be crumbly. Spoon batter over apples in pan. Dot with butter; sprinkle with cinnamon and top with pecans. Bake at 375 degrees for 30 to 40 minutes, until a toothpick inserted in the center tests clean. Serve warm, topped with whipped cream or ice cream. Makes 12 servings.

Baking together is a fun family activity...a great choice for kids just starting to learn how to cook. As you measure and mix, be sure to share any stories about hand-me-down recipes. You'll be creating memories as well as sweet treats!

Chocolate Blueberry Snack Cake

Maegan Stauffer
Findlay, OH

I love the simple ingredients in this recipe. I adapted a fudge cake recipe to lighten it up for summer picnics. It's scrumptious anytime!

1 c. boiling water
1 t. baking soda
1 c. all-purpose flour
1 c. sugar
1/4 c. baking cocoa
1/4 c. butter, sliced
2 T. brewed coffee, cooled
1 egg, beaten
1/2 c. fresh blueberries
Garnish: powdered sugar

Combine boiling water and baking soda in a cup; set aside. In a large bowl, combine flour, sugar and baking cocoa; mix well. Add butter and baking soda mixture; stir until butter is melted. Add coffee and egg; mix well. Fold in blueberries. Pour batter into a greased 8"x8" glass baking pan. Bake at 350 degrees for 30 to 35 minutes, until cake tests done. Sprinkle with powdered sugar while still warm; cut into squares. Makes 9 to 12 servings.

For best results when baking, let butter stand at room temperature at least 30 minutes before using. Short on time? Speed things up by grating chilled sticks of butter with a cheese grater.

Easy-as-Pie DESSERTS

Simple Cherry Squares

Diane Bertosa
Brunswick Hills, OH

This recipe was given to me by a high school classmate over 50 years ago. It is a family favorite! Any flavor of pie filling can be used...we like cherry, but blueberry works well too.

1 c. butter
2 c. all-purpose flour
1 c. sugar
2 eggs, beaten
1 t. vanilla
21-oz. can cherry pie filling

In a large bowl, stir butter until softened. Mix in flour, sugar, eggs and vanilla; stir until a dough forms. Spread dough in a lightly greased 13"x9" baking pan. Spread pie filling on top. Bake at 350 degrees for 35 to 40 minutes. Cut into squares. Makes 12 servings.

Apricot Bars

Sandy Ward
Anderson, IN

Oh-so simple to make! Great for Mothers' Day showers and tea parties, or anytime you want a fruity treat.

1-1/2 c. all-purpose flour
3/4 c. brown sugar, packed
6 T. margarine, softened
3/4 c. apricot preserves

Combine flour, brown sugar and margarine in a bowl; mix together until well blended. Pat half of dough into a greased 9"x9" baking pan. Spread preserves on top; add remaining flour mixture and pat lightly. Bake at 350 degrees for about 30 minutes. Cool; cut into bars. Makes 10 to 12 servings.

A party without cake is really just a meeting.
–Julia Child

Chocolate-Peanut Saltine Toffee

Sharon Theisen
St. Cloud, MN

Everyone loves these...they're the most-requested treat at gatherings!

1 sleeve saltine crackers
1 c. butter, sliced
1 c. brown sugar, packed
2 T. honey
1-1/4 c. semi-sweet chocolate chips
1 c. peanuts, finely chopped

Arrange saltine crackers in a single layer in a parchment paper-lined 13"x9" baking pan; set aside. In a saucepan, melt butter over medium heat. Add brown sugar and honey; whisk to blend well. Cook and stir until mixture is simmering and brown sugar is dissolved. Remove from heat; allow to cool for 2 to 3 minutes, until slightly thickened. Immediately spoon over crackers in pan. Bake at 375 degrees for 5 to 6 minutes. Remove from oven; cool for 5 minutes. Meanwhile, melt chocolate chips according to package directions. Dollop melted chocolate over crackers; use a spatula to smooth the top. Sprinkle with peanuts. Refrigerate until cooled and set; break into pieces and serve. Makes 2 dozen.

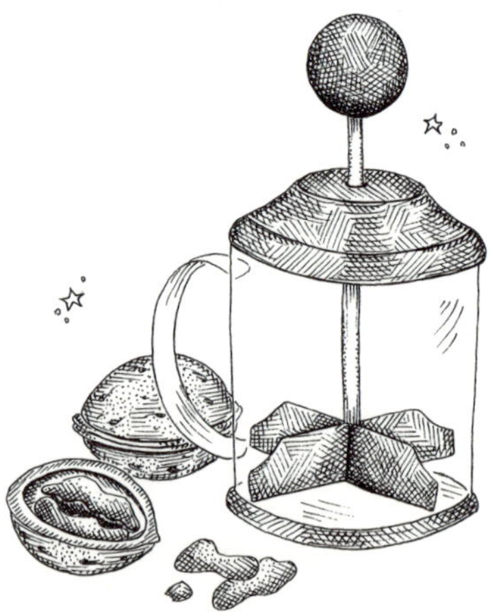

An old-fashioned food chopper quickly chops small quantities of nuts for cookie recipes. Safe for kids to use, too!

Easy-as-Pie DESSERTS

Little Rock Cakes

Eve Travis
Fort Pierce, FL

I love to cook! I started cooking when I was seven and now I am 16. I have a special apron to wear every time I am cooking. I made up this recipe when I was younger, and I have used and loved it ever since. I like to deliver cookies to our neighbors.

1-1/2 c. all-purpose flour
1 c. brown sugar, packed
2 eggs, beaten
1 t. baking powder
1 t. vanilla extract
Garnish: sugar

Mix together all ingredients except garnish in a bowl. Roll dough into one-inch balls; arrange on parchment paper-lined baking sheets. Bake at 350 degrees for 8 to 10 minutes. Sprinkle cookies with sugar as they cool. Makes about one dozen.

Aunt Tookie's Cake Mix Cookies

Jennifer Gaudet
Richmond Hill, GA

My aunt gave this cookie recipe to my mom, many years ago. They're so easy to make, and the flavor possibilities are endless! Dress 'em up with canned frosting and some sprinkles.

15-1/4 oz. pkg. cake mix, any flavor
1/2 c. butter, softened
1 egg, beaten
1 t. vanilla extract

Combine all ingredients in a large bowl; mix together by hand. Form dough into one-inch balls by teaspoonfuls; arrange on ungreased baking sheets, 2 inches apart. Bake at 350 degrees for 8 to 10 minutes, until golden. Cool on baking sheets for a few minutes; transfer to wire racks. Makes 2 to 3 dozen.

Keep ingredients on hand for a yummy, quick-fix dessert. A real life-saver whenever your child announces, "Mom, there's a bake sale...tomorrow!"

Pumpkin Dessert

Dorothy Bussart
Wichita, KS

This dessert is wonderful! I'm in my 90s and still baking.

15-oz. can pumpkin
12-oz. can evaporated milk
3 eggs, beaten
1 c. sugar
2 t. cinnamon
2 t. pumpkin pie spice
15-1/4 oz. pkg. yellow cake mix
1/4 c. butter, melted
8-oz. container frozen whipped topping, thawed

In a large bowl, combine pumpkin, evaporated milk, eggs, sugar and spices. Mix well; spoon batter into a greased 13"x9" baking pan. Crumble dry cake mix on top; drizzle melted butter evenly over all. Bake at 350 degrees for one hour; cool. Serve with whipped topping. Makes 10 to 12 servings.

Dreamy Butter Cookies

Melanie Springer
Canton, OH

These cherry-topped cookies look so pretty on holiday cookie trays.

1 c. butter, softened
1/2 c. sugar
2-1/4 c. all-purpose flour
1 t. almond extract
1/4 t. salt
10-oz. jar maraschino cherries, well drained and cut in half, if desired

In a large bowl, stir butter until softened; gradually stir in sugar. Blend well. Blend in flour, extract and salt. Shape dough into balls by tablespoonfuls; arrange on ungreased baking sheets. Press a whole or half cherry into each cookie, allowing cherry to show slightly. Bake at 350 degrees for about 8 to 9 minutes, until lightly golden. Cool on a wire rack. Makes 2 to 2-1/2 dozen.

A touch of whimsy...use Grandma's old cow-shaped cream pitcher to top desserts with sauce.

Easy-as-Pie DESSERTS

Soft Sugared Gingerbread

Judy Henfey
Cibolo, TX

I received this recipe from a co-worker at my bridal shower in 1987. It's still a great recipe...simple and delicious! Great at Christmas... good any time of the year. Serve with a cup of hot coffee.

1 c. whole milk
1 t. baking soda
1 c. butter, softened
2 c. sugar
2 eggs
3 c. all-purpose flour
1 t. salt
1 t. ground ginger
cinnamon-sugar to taste
Garnish: whipped cream

Combine milk and baking soda in a cup; stir well and set aside. In a large bowl, blend together butter and sugar. Add eggs, one at a time; mix well and set aside. In another bowl, combine flour, salt and ginger. Add flour mixture to butter mixture alternately with milk mixture; stir until well combined. Spread batter in a greased 13"x9" baking pan; sprinkle with cinnamon-sugar. Bake at 325 degrees for 40 minutes. Cool; cut into squares. Serve topped with whipped cream. Makes 10 to 12 servings.

You're never too old to enjoy a tea party! Make iced cookies and sugar-dusted cakes, and fill dainty cups with spiced tea... a delightful way to spend an afternoon with friends.

Grammie's Chocolate Chip Cookies

Jenni Ritchie
Scotts Valley, CA

This is my grandma's recipe. She taught me how to cook and bake, and I have the best memories of being in her kitchen with her. She loved Gooseberry Patch and I wanted to honor her memory by sharing her cookie recipe. I miss her everyday.

3/4 c. butter-flavored shortening
1-1/4 c. light brown sugar, packed
1 egg, beaten
2 T. milk
1 T. vanilla extract
2 c. all-purpose flour
3/4 t. baking soda
1/2 t. salt
2 to 3 c. semi-sweet chocolate chips

In a large bowl, beat shortening and brown sugar together with an electric mixer on medium speed until well blended. Add egg, milk and vanilla; beat well. Gradually mix in flour, baking soda and salt; fold in chocolate chips. Drop dough by tablespoonfuls onto parchment paper-lined baking sheets. Bake at 375 degrees for 10 to 11 minutes. Remove cookies to a wire rack to cool. Makes 16 cookies.

A small scoop is so handy when making drop cookies. Just scoop the dough from the bowl and release it onto the baking sheet. Perfect portions every time!

Easy-as-Pie DESSERTS

Butterscotch Cookies

Kathy Scott
Corbin, KY

These cookies are addictive!You just can't walk by the cookie platter without eating one or two.

15-1/4 oz. pkg. yellow cake mix
2 eggs, beaten
1/2 c. oil
1 t. vanilla extract
1-1/2 c. flaked coconut
1 c. chopped pecans
6-oz. pkg. butterscotch baking chips

In a large bowl, whisk together dry cake mix, eggs, oil and vanilla. Add remaining ingredients and mix until thoroughly combined. Using a one-inch scoop, scoop dough and roll slightly by hand into round balls. Arrange on parchment paper-lined baking sheets. Bake at 350 degrees for about 12 to 13 minutes. Remove to a wire rack to cool. Store in a covered container. Makes 2 dozen.

If you're pressed for time, mix up cookie dough, pop it in the refrigerator, and bake later when guests arrive. They'll love the aroma of fresh-baked cookies!

Fresh Strawberry Pie

Sandra Paulin
Bloomington, IN

My mother always made fresh strawberry pie for Memorial Day. I carried on the tradition, and since our twins were born in May on Mothers' Day weekend, we celebrated their birthday with fresh strawberry pie. Our grandchildren now enjoy this pie too.

2 9-inch pie crusts, unbaked
2-1/2 c. plus 5 T. water, divided
1-1/2 c. sugar
5 T. cornstarch
6-oz. pkg. strawberry gelatin mix
4 c. fresh strawberries, hulled and sliced
Optional: whipped topping

Bake pie crusts at 450 degrees for 10 to 12 minutes; set aside to cool. Meanwhile, in a large saucepan, mix together 2-1/2 cups water and sugar; bring to a boil. In a small cup, mix cornstarch with enough of remaining water to make a liquid. Stir into hot water mixture, stirring well until thickened. Add dry gelatin mix and stir well. Remove from heat and cool; add strawberries and mix well. Divide strawberry mixture between crusts; cover and refrigerate until set. Cut into wedges; serve topped with whipped topping, if desired. Makes 2 pies; each serves 8.

Whipped cream is a must with homemade desserts. Save time...pick up an aerosol can of sweetened whipped cream and dollop away!

Easy-as-Pie DESSERTS

Raspberry Bars

Irene Robinson
Cincinnati, OH

Everyone who has tried these cookie bars loves them. They look great on a cookie tray, too! They freeze nicely.

1 c. butter, softened
1 c. sugar
2 egg yolks, beaten
1 t. vanilla extract
2 c. all-purpose flour
3/4 to 1 c. raspberry preserves
1 c. chopped nuts
Garnish: powdered sugar

Combine butter, sugar and egg yolks in a large bowl; stir until well blended. Add vanilla and flour; mix well. Pat half of dough into a greased 9"x9" baking pan. Spread preserves over dough; crumble remaining dough over preserves. Sprinkle with nuts. Bake at 350 degrees for 30 to 35 minutes. Cool on a wire rack; sprinkle with powdered sugar and cut into squares.

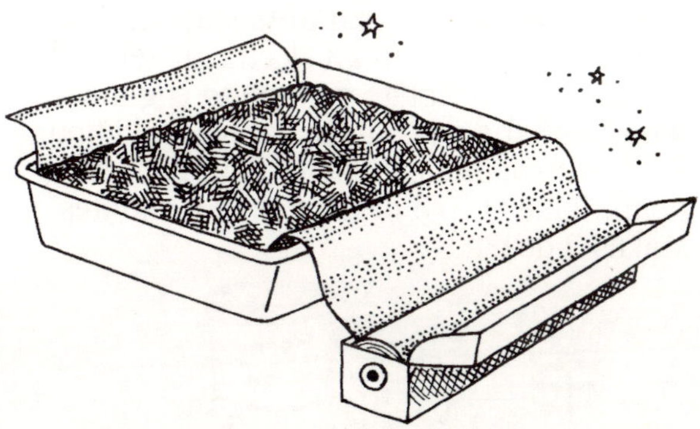

Make perfect bar cookies. Lay a length of aluminum foil across the baking pan, extending a few inches on each side. Grease, fill and bake as directed. Use the extra foil as handles to lift out the cooled, baked cookies onto a cutting board. Cut neatly into squares.

Mom's Brownies

Janae Mallonee
Maynard, MA

These are the brownies I grew up on. They are gooey, chocolatey and will completely ruin any diet you ever considered. Mother and I have a lifelong brownie battle going. She feels all brownies should have walnuts, whereas I feel like that is the most horrible thing you could ever do to such a delicious food. The solution? Whoever made them got to decide! Sometimes one of us would be nice and make the batter half and half...sometimes. Whenever I make a batch of them, I'm amazed at how quickly I'm transported back to my childhood! The smell is just such a trigger. I don't mind....the six-year-old me doesn't have all these adult responsibilities. Being six again for a minute is great!

8-oz. pkg. unsweetened baking chocolate, broken up
1 c. butter
5 eggs, beaten
3 c. sugar
1 T. vanilla extract
1-1/2 c. all-purpose flour
Optional: 2 c. chopped walnuts

Combine chocolate pieces and butter in a microwave-safe bowl. Microwave on high for 2 minutes; stir until smooth. In a large bowl, combine eggs and sugar; beat with an electric mixer on high speed for 2 minutes. Gradually add chocolate mixture to egg mixture, a little at a time to begin with, then the rest. Stir in vanilla. Add flour, 1/2 cup at time; mix well. Fold in walnuts, if using. Pour batter into a greased 13"x9" baking pan. Bake at 375 degrees for 35 minutes. Cool and cut into squares. Makes 2 dozen.

Invite family & friends to an old-fashioned ice cream social! Set out tubs of ice cream and lots of toppings...ripe bananas, peanuts, maraschino cherries, hot fudge sauce and fluffy whipped cream. And of course, plenty of napkins!

Easy-as-Pie DESSERTS

Mary's Fudge Brownie Icing

Pat Beach
Fisherville, KY

My sister Mary loves anything chocolate and decided a layer of fudge on top of brownies would be heavenly. She was right! You'll never eat plain brownies again, after you top your brownies with this icing.

1-1/2 c. sugar
6 T. butter
6 T. milk
1 c. milk chocolate chips
1 t. vanilla extract
Optional: 1/2 c. chopped nuts

In a heavy saucepan over medium heat, combine sugar, butter and milk. Stir together and bring to a boil. Once it comes to a boil, allow it to boil for 30 seconds. Remove from heat. Add chocolate chips, vanilla and nuts, if using. Stir quickly until chocolate chips are melted; spoon over warm brownies. Let icing set up before cutting brownies. Serves 8 to 10.

Buttercream Cake Frosting

Karen Wilson
Defiance, OH

Of all of my recipes, this is the one recipe my kids and grandkids ask for the most. I use this delectable frosting for cakes, cookies and cinnamon rolls.

1/2 c. butter
1/2 c. shortening
4 c. powdered sugar
1/4 t. salt
1 t. vanilla extract
1/4 c. milk

Stir butter and shortening in a bowl until well blended. Add remaining ingredients and mix until smooth; do not overmix. Makes enough frosting to frost one cake.

Life is uncertain. Eat dessert first.

– Ernestine Ulmer

Hasty Peach Cobbler

Trudy Satterwhite
San Antonio, TX

An all-time favorite! Super-simple to make, simply delicious to eat.

1/4 c. butter
1/2 c. sugar
1 c. all-purpose flour
2 t. baking powder
1/4 t. salt
1/2 c. milk
21-oz. can peach pie filling

Beat butter and sugar in a large bowl until light and fluffy. Stir in flour, baking powder and salt alternately with milk; beat until smooth. Pour batter into a lightly greased 8"x8" baking pan. Spoon pie filling over batter. Bake at 350 degrees for 30 minutes, or until golden. Serve warm. Makes 6 servings.

Keep a variety of fruit pie fillings and cake mixes in the pantry for delicious desserts anytime.

Easy-as-Pie DESSERTS

Cherry Pie Bubble-Up

Tina Goodpasture
Meadowview, VA

Want a quick & easy treat that is so sweet? This is it!

21-oz. can cherry pie filling
16.3-oz. tube refrigerated jumbo biscuits, quartered
1/2 c. powdered sugar
1 T. milk

Pour pie filling into a large bowl. Add biscuit pieces; stir gently to coat. Spoon mixture into a 13"x9" baking pan coated with non-stick vegetable spray; spread out biscuits in pan. Bake at 350 degrees for 30 minutes. In a small bowl, mix together powered sugar and milk. Drizzle over slightly cooled dessert and serve. Makes 8 servings.

Gilda's Strawberry Dessert

Mary Rabon
Mobile, AL

This recipe started with my grandmother, and then my cousin and dear friend Gilda started making it for family parties. Now I make it for my family and they love it too! It is light and refreshing...great for summer, and for the Fourth of July! The recipe can easily be halved for fewer servings.

2 3-oz. pkgs. strawberry gelatin mix
3 c. boiling water
3 c. cold water
1/2 to 1 bakery angel food cake, torn into pieces
2 16-oz. pkgs. fresh strawberries, hulled and sliced
16-oz. container frozen whipped topping, thawed

In a large bowl, stir together gelatin mixes and boiling water until dissolved. Add cold water; refrigerate until slightly jelled. In a large glass trifle bowl, layer 1/3 each of cake pieces, strawberries, gelatin and whipped topping. Layer 2 more times, ending with topping. Cover and chill for one hour or more. Makes 10 to 12 servings.

Pick up an extra set of measuring spoons...you'll never need to stop in the middle of a recipe to wash spoons!

Caramel Apple Crisp

Sarah Slaven
Strunk, KY

This is one of our favorite desserts...I make it often throughout the autumn season. It's even better made with home-canned apple pie filling!

1-3/4 c. all-purpose flour
1 c. quick-cooking oats, uncooked
1/2 c. brown sugar, packed
1/2 t. baking soda
1/2 t. salt
1 c. cold butter
20 caramels, unwrapped
14-oz. can sweetened condensed milk
21-oz. can apple pie filling
Garnish: vanilla ice cream

In a large bowl, combine flour, oats, brown sugar, baking soda and salt. Cut in butter with a pastry blender or fork until crumbly; set aside 1-1/2 cups crumb mixture. Press remaining crumb mixture into a greased 13"x9" baking pan to form a crust. Bake at 375 degrees for 15 minutes. Meanwhile, melt caramels in a saucepan over low heat. Gradually add condensed milk; cook and stir until smooth. Spoon pie filling over baked crust; top with caramel mixture. Sprinkle with reserved crumb mixture. Bake at 375 degrees for 20 minutes; let cool. Serve warm, topped with a scoop of ice cream. Makes 6 servings.

For a toasty, nutty flavor, bake oats before they're used in recipes. Simply spread them on a baking sheet and bake for 10 to 12 minutes at 300 degrees. Cool slightly before using.

Easy-as-Pie DESSERTS

Mom's Low-Fat Cheesecake

Mary Ann Dell
Phoenixville, PA

A favorite recipe from Mom. It's the most delicious cheesecake to make, and it's low-fat, too. Perfect to serve for any occasion.

3 8-oz. pkgs. Neufchâtel cheese, softened
3 eggs, beaten
1 c. sugar
1 T . vanilla extract
3 c. low-fat sour cream
Optional: fruit topping or pie filling

Combine Neufchâtel cheese, eggs, sugar and vanilla in a large bowl. Beat with an electric mixer on low to medium speed until smooth. Blend in sour cream; beat for 5 minutes. Spoon into a greased and floured 10" round springform pan. Bake at 325 degrees for one hour. Cover and chill for 4 to 5 hours. Remove sides of pan; serve plain or with fruit topping. Serves 12.

Mandarin Cream Pie

Kimberly Trotter
Monroe, MI

This recipe was handed down to me by my mother-in-law, because it was a favorite of my soon-to-be husband. It is simple and requires little prep time. We now have this pie often for holidays and gatherings. This recipe is very versatile and sure to get your creativity kickstarted! Try it with maraschino cherries and pecans, instead of oranges and walnuts. Yum!

8-oz. container frozen whipped topping, thawed
1/2 c. cream cheese, softened
8-oz. pkg. chopped walnuts
15-oz. can mandarin oranges, well drained
9-inch graham cracker crust

In a large bowl, blend whipped topping and cream cheese until well combined. Fold in walnuts; fold in oranges. Spoon mixture into graham cracker crust. Serve immediately, or cover and refrigerate to serve later. Makes 8 servings.

For the tastiest desserts of all kinds, nothing beats real butter!

Ice Cream Sandwich Cake

Amy Butcher
Columbus, GA

A scrumptious no-bake dessert that's perfect for parties, and so easy to make. Decorate it with candy sprinkles, just for fun.

24 vanilla ice cream sandwiches, unwrapped and divided
2 8-oz. containers frozen whipped topping, thawed and divided
12-oz. jar hot fudge ice cream topping, warmed and divided
12-oz. jar caramel ice cream topping, warmed and divided
1/4 c. chopped pecans

Arrange half of ice cream sandwiches in a 13"x9" glass baking pan, cutting sandwiches to fit, if needed. Top evenly with half each of whipped topping, fudge topping and caramel topping. Repeat layering, ending with whipped topping. Sprinkle with pecans. Cover and freeze until set, about 30 minutes. Cut into squares and serve. Makes 12 to 15 servings.

Save the sprinkles! Before adding candy sprinkles to cookies or desserts, cover the table with a length of wax paper. Return any excess sprinkles to their jars by simply folding the paper in half, gently shaking sprinkles to one side and tipping them into the jar.

Easy-as-Pie DESSERTS

Sweet & Salty Peanut Butter Cookies

Jamie Derr
Branson, MO

This simple flourless, gluten-free cookie recipe is always a hit! I've heard, "This is the best peanut butter cookie I've ever had!" more times than I can count. Using brown sugar adds a chewy texture to the cookie, and a sprinkle of coarse salt on the top makes for the perfect sweet & salty treat.

1 c. creamy peanut butter
1 c. brown sugar, packed
1 egg, beaten
2 t. vanilla extract
Garnish: coarse sea salt to taste

Combine peanut butter, brown sugar, egg and vanilla in a bowl. Beat with an electric mixer on medium speed until well blended. Cover and chill dough until firm. Using a small cookie scoop, drop dough by tablespoonfuls onto parchment paper-lined baking sheets. Flatten cookies with a fork, criss-crossing for a classic peanut butter cookie look. Top with a sprinkle of sea salt. Bake at 350 degrees for 12 to 14 minutes. Cool cookies on a wire rack. Makes one dozen.

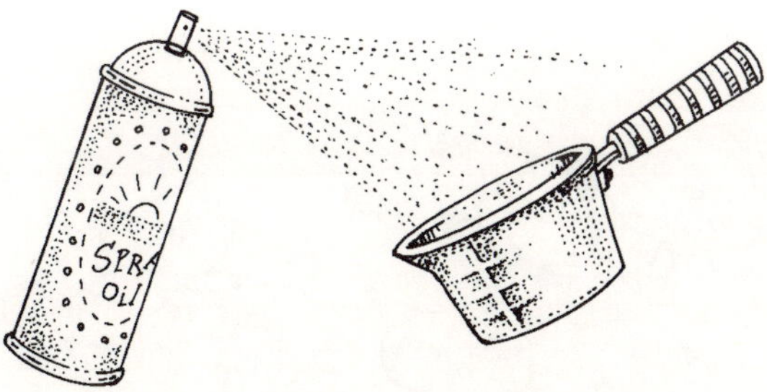

When measuring peanut butter or honey, spray the measuring cup with non-stick vegetable spray first. The contents will slip right out!

Cream-Filled Crispy Rice Bars

Vicki Van Donselaar
Cedar, IA

These are basically Scotcheroos with a cream filling...yum! They are a hit with our youth group kids and I don't have many left over whenever I make a batch of these.

1 c. corn syrup
1 c. brown sugar, packed
2-1/4 c. creamy peanut butter, divided
4 c. crispy rice cereal
1/2 c. butter, melted
6 T. milk
1/4 c. instant vanilla pudding mix
4 c. powdered sugar
1-1/2 c. semi-sweet chocolate chips

In a large saucepan, combine corn syrup, brown sugar and 2 cups peanut butter over medium-low heat. Cook and stir until well blended; add cereal and mix well. Press into a buttered 15"x10" jelly-roll pan; cover and chill. In a large bowl, mix melted butter, milk and dry pudding mix. Add powdered sugar; beat until smooth. Spoon over cereal mixture in pan; cover and chill. Melt chocolate chips with remaining peanut butter in a small saucepan over low heat. Stir well and spread over chilled mixture. Chill again; cut into squares. Makes 2 dozen.

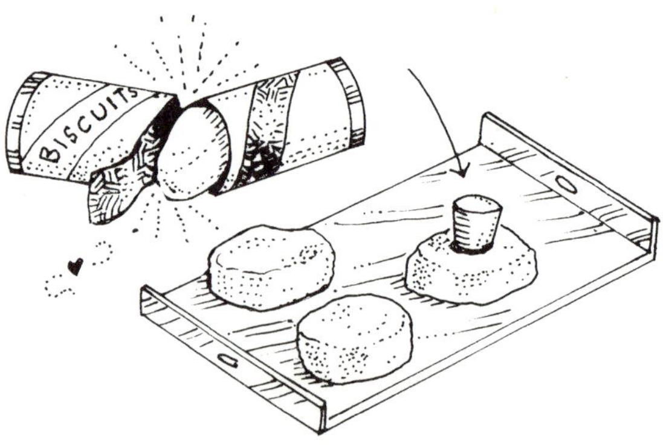

Doughnuts in a dash...scrumptious any time of day! Separate refrigerated biscuits and cut a hole in the center of each. Fry biscuits in hot oil until golden on both sides; drain on paper towels. Roll in sugar and serve warm.

Easy-as-Pie DESSERTS

Citrus Shortbread Cookies

Reenie & Angie Salayon
New Orleans, LA

We love shortbread, but sometimes find it a bit too heavy and buttery tasting. This bit of lemon makes it a great light treat with coffee or tea, especially in the warmer months!

1/2 c. butter, softened
3/4 c. superfine sugar
2 egg yolks
2 c. all-purpose flour
zest of 1 lemon

In a bowl, beat softened butter with sugar until light and fluffy. Beat in egg yolks, one at a time, until thoroughly blended. Add flour and lemon zest; stir to make a stiff dough. Knead dough lightly on a floured surface. Roll out to about 1/4-inch thick. Cut out dough using a 3" round cookie cutter; arrange on buttered or parchment paper-lined baking sheets. Bake at 350 degrees for about 15 minutes, or until firm and lightly golden. Transfer to a wire rack; cool completely. Makes 1-1/2 dozen.

No-Bake Brownies

Lisa Barger
Conroe, TX

This is a fun and easy recipe to make with the kids!

1 T. butter, softened
1 c. finely chopped nuts, divided
2 1-oz. sqs. unsweetened baking chocolate
14-oz. can sweetened condensed milk
2 to 2-1/2 c. vanilla wafer crumbs

Coat a 9"x9" baking pan with butter. Sprinkle 1/4 cup nuts evenly in pan; set aside. In a heavy saucepan over low heat, melt chocolate with condensed milk. Cook and stir until mixture thickens, about 10 minutes. Remove from heat. Stir in vanilla wafer crumbs and 1/4 cup nuts. Spread evenly in pan. Top with remaining nuts. Cover and chill until firm, 3 or 4 hours. Cut into squares. Makes 2 dozen.

Pig-Pickin' Cake

Sarah Bray
Richmond, KY

This luscious cake is very easy to make...sure to be welcome at any family gathering or potluck!

15-1/4 oz. pkg. yellow cake mix
1/4 c. oil
4 eggs, beaten
11-oz. can mandarin oranges
20-oz. can crushed pineapple, drained
3-1/2 oz. pkg. instant vanilla pudding mix
8-oz. container frozen whipped topping, thawed
Optional: 1/2 to 1 c. crushed pecans or walnuts

Combine dry cake mix, oil, eggs and undrained mandarin oranges in a large bowl. Beat with an electric mixer on medium speed for 2 minutes. Spoon batter into a greased 13"x9" baking pan. Bake at 350 degrees for 35 to 40 minutes. Cool cake completely; may cool in refrigerator, if needed. In another bowl, add pineapple, dry pudding mix, whipped topping and nuts, if desired; fold together until completely combined. Spread over cooled cake. Cool and refrigerate until ready to serve. Cut into squares. Serves 10 to 12.

Nothing hits the spot like a hot cup of coffee alongside dessert! Pamper coffee lovers with fresh cream, turbinado sugar and honey.

Easy-as-Pie DESSERTS

Best-Ever Banana Pudding

Cassie Hooker
La Porte, TX

My kids love this banana pudding! It is very light and fluffy.

14-oz. can sweetened condensed milk
1-1/2 c. cold water
3.4-oz. pkg. instant banana pudding mix
2 c. whipping cream
11-oz. pkg. vanilla wafers
3 to 4 ripe bananas, sliced

In a large bowl, beat together condensed milk, cold water and dry pudding mix with an electric mixer on medium speed until well blended; chill for 5 minutes. In a separate bowl, using clean beaters, beat cream on medium-high speed until fluffy. Fold whipped cream into pudding mixture. Layer 1/3 of vanilla wafers in a 3-quart casserole dish; add 1/3 of pudding mixture and 1/3 of bananas. Repeat, making 2 more layers. If desired, reserve some wafers and banana slices to garnish top of pudding. Cover and chill for several hours before serving. Makes 12 servings.

Evaporated milk and sweetened condensed milk are both useful in all kinds of scrumptious desserts...but they aren't interchangeable. Condensed milk contains sugar and is cooked down to a thickened consistency, while evaporated milk has no added sugar. Check the can for recipe success!

Mocha Tortoni

Sharlene Reid
British Columbia, Canada

My mom found the recipe for this frozen dessert in a magazine years ago, and like women of her generation (and even me!), she cut out and saved these recipes that became family favorites. I've never seen this recipe anywhere else. Enjoy!

1 c. chocolate wafers, crushed and divided
1 pt. chocolate ice cream
2 t. instant coffee granules
1/2 c. chopped pecans
1/4 c. semi-sweet chocolate chips

Set 12 paper baking cups in a muffin tin. Set aside half of chocolate wafer crumbs for topping; divide remaining crumbs among muffin cups. Set aside. Add ice cream to a small chilled bowl. Add coffee granules; stir with a wooden spoon, working quickly to soften but not melt ice cream. Fold in pecans and chocolate chips; spoon quickly into muffin cups. Sprinkle with reserved wafer crumbs. Freeze until serving time. Makes 6 servings.

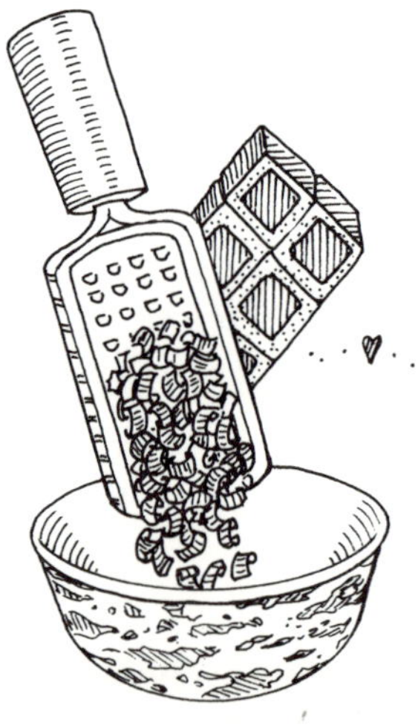

Chocolate shavings are a great way to garnish desserts! They're simple to create using a microplane grater or vegetable peeler.

Easy-as-Pie DESSERTS

Heavenly Angel Dessert

Judy Lange
Imperial, PA

Company is coming and you need a quick dessert! I can whip this up in no time. It's a perfect ending after a delicious meal from my favorite **Gooseberry Patch** *cookbook.*

8-oz. pkg. cream cheese, softened
1 c. powdered sugar
8-oz. container frozen whipped topping, thawed
14-oz. bakery angel food cake, cut into 1-inch cubes
1 to 2 21-oz. cans blueberry pie filling

In a large bowl, beat together cream cheese and powdered sugar. Fold in whipped topping and cake cubes; spread evenly into a 13"x9" baking pan. Top with pie filling. Cover and refrigerate for at least 2 hours or overnight. Cut into squares. Serves 12.

Sundae Cake

Angie Biggin
Lyons, IL

A special dessert that I can stir up in a jiffy!

15-1/4 oz. pkg. chocolate or devil's food cake mix
12-oz. jar caramel topping
16-oz. container frozen whipped topping, thawed
1 chocolate-caramel peanut candy bar, chopped

Prepare cake mix according to package directions; bake in a greased 13"x9" baking pan. Poke holes in the top of still-warm cake with a wooden spoon handle. Pour caramel topping into holes in cake; allow to cool. Spread whipped topping over cake; sprinkle with chopped candy bar. Cover and refrigerate. Makes 12 to 15 servings.

Make dessert a grand finale... serve it on your prettiest china plates!

Wacky Cake

Pam Hooley
LaGrange, IN

I have been making this chocolate cake ever since I started baking, around the age of ten. It is simple, delicious and very quick to get into the oven. Once, I even made it for a wedding cake! It's a great one to decorate, as it does not crumb. You can use coffee instead of water if you want a richer taste. This cake needs no frosting, but a dusting of powdered sugar looks nice.

3 c. all-purpose flour
2 c. sugar
1/2 c. baking cocoa
2 t. baking soda
1 t. salt
2 c. water
2/3 c. oil
2 T. vinegar
2 t. vanilla extract

Combine all ingredients in a large bowl; mix well by hand. Pour batter into a greased 13"x9" baking pan. Bake at 350 degrees for 30 minutes, or until a toothpick inserted in the center comes out clean. Cool; cut into squares. Serves 12 to 15.

Reach into Grandma's recipe box for that extra-special cake you remember...and then bake it to share with the whole family. If you don't have her recipe box, maybe you'll spot that same recipe in a *Gooseberry Patch* cookbook!

Easy-as-Pie DESSERTS

Chocolatey Cookie Pie

Kathy Grashoff
Fort Wayne, IN

This recipe is easy and oh-so good! It will speed you along for the holidays...the pie crust takes it over the top! Plus, it freezes beautifully, so you'll have it handy when you're busy.

2 eggs
1/2 c. brown sugar, packed
1/4 c. sugar
1/2 c. all-purpose flour
1 c. semi-sweet chocolate chips
1/2 c. butter, melted and slightly cooled
9-inch pie crust, unbaked
Garnish: vanilla ice cream

In a large bowl, whisk eggs until foamy. Mix in sugars and flour. Slowly stir in chocolate chips and melted butter. Pour batter into unbaked pie crust. Bake at 325 degrees for about one hour. Cut into wedges and serve warm, topped with a scoop of ice cream. Makes 6 to 8 servings.

Serve ice cream-topped desserts to a party crowd, the quick & easy way! Scoop the ice cream ahead of time and freeze in muffin cups.

INDEX

Beverages

Breads

Breakfasts

Cookies

Desserts

Mains

INDEX

Salads

Sandwiches

Sides

INDEX

Snacks & Appetizers

Soups

more time for fun the perfect meal

slowly simmered 'round the table

sweet & savory home cooking

flavorful favorites oh-so easy

U.S. to Metric Recipe Equivalents

Volume Measurements

1/4 teaspoon	1 mL
1/2 teaspoon	2 mL
1 teaspoon	5 mL
1 tablespoon = 3 teaspoons	15 mL
2 tablespoons = 1 fluid ounce	30 mL
1/4 cup	60 mL
1/3 cup	75 mL
1/2 cup = 4 fluid ounces	125 mL
1 cup = 8 fluid ounces	250 mL
2 cups = 1 pint =16 fluid ounces	500 mL
4 cups = 1 quart	1 L

Weights

1 ounce	30 g
4 ounces	120 g
8 ounces	225 g
16 ounces = 1 pound	450 g

Oven Temperatures

300° F	150° C
325° F	160° C
350° F	180° C
375° F	190° C
400° F	200° C
450° F	230° C

Baking Pan Sizes

Square

8x8x2 inches	2 L = 20x20x5 cm
9x9x2 inches	2.5 L = 23x23x5 cm

Rectangular

13x9x2 inches	3.5 L = 33x23x5 cm

Loaf

9x5x3 inches	2 L = 23x13x7 cm

Round

8x1-1/2 inches	1.2 L = 20x4 cm
9x1-1/2 inches	1.5 L = 23x4 cm